Roman, Sax and Viking Ti

Jo Lawrie & Paul Noble

Collins Educational

SKILLS AND RESOURCES FOR HISTORY

Design and typesetting by Brian Green Associates
Picture Research by Valerie Randall
Illustrations by Sheila Cant
Printed in Great Britain

Acknowledgements

Every effort has been made to contact the holders of copyright material but if any have
been inadvertently overlooked, the publishers will be pleased to make the necessary
arrangements at the first opportunity.
The authors and publishers would like to thank the following for permission to use photographs
and documents:
Battle of Maldon (upper extract) from Laborde, E.D., *Byrhtnoth and Maldon*, London,
William Heinemann Ltd, 1936
Battle of Maldon (lower extract) from Bone, Gavin, *Anglo-Saxon Poetry*, Oxford, Clarendon Press, 1944
by permission of Oxford University Press 64
C.M.Dixon Photo Resources 91, 94
e.t.archive 53, 66
English Heritage Photo Library 31
Robert Harding Picture Library 36, 37, 40
Michael Holford 41
The Mansell Collection Ltd 24, 38, 41, 42, 95
Museum of London 40, 45
Musée national du Bardo 44
Ronald Sheridan/The Ancient Art and Architecture Collection 30, 37, 38, 40, 42, 45, 80, 94
St Edmundsbury Borough Council/West Stow Anglo-Saxon Village Trust 57
Trustees of the British Museum 45
University Museum of National Antiquities, Oslo, Norway 79
York Archaeological Trust Historical Picture Library 80, 82, 94

Cover photographs:
Werner Foundation (Viking ship);
Trinity College Library, Dublin (Manuscript);
English Heritage Photo Library (Model of Legionary soldier, Hadrian's Wall)

Contents

Introduction

'Romans, Anglo-Saxons and Vikings in Britain', the Key Stage 2 Study Unit of national curriculum history, to which this book relates, covers 1000 years from 55BC to the early part of the eleventh century. When approaching a topic, which covers such a large swathe of time, one is bound to encounter simplifications and constraints not present in a topic such as 'Britain Since 1930' which covers barely 70 years. Even the language used to describe the period varies widely.

In Roman, Saxon and Viking times Britain was under constant attack from predatory invaders who, by brute force, pushed the indigenous Celtic peoples back into the more inhospitable corners of these islands. But these invaders were also settlers, a title which somehow puts them in a more kindly light. They were simply people looking for places to colonise, and land where they could raise families and grow food to feed them. Whether we regard them as invaders or as settlers, there is a tendency to judge each group differently.

The Romans are generally regarded as civilising and benign (you must forget Boudica's daughters), whereas the Vikings are seen as brutal and barbaric.

The Romans did indeed bring Britain within the influence of the civilised world but when the Romans departed, a so-called 'Dark Age' descended. Barbarian hordes from the north and east ravaged the land 'with fire and sword', before establishing their primitive (by Roman standards) settlements. But the so-called Dark Age appears dark more as a result of the lack of historical knowledge about the period (only a small group of texts, annals and fragments exist for the fifth and sixth centuries) and pro-classical prejudices, than anything else.

Though the arguments about the positive and negative effects of the successive invasions are academic, this does not preclude young children from appreciating the debate. They can learn about the positive values and skills of each invading group as well as about their more barbarous behaviour. Clearly these people shaped British society in fundamental and lasting ways, and this fact alone makes them worthy of study. Through place-names, language, dialects, patterns of settlement and even the national gene bank, they have left a significant legacy to our own times.

Teaching this unit

First the study of a thousand years of history must be made manageable. The whole can only be dealt with in outline and the national curriculum directs that this outline should deal with:

a the Roman conquest and occupation of Britain

b the arrival and settlement of the Anglo-Saxons

c Viking raids and settlements.

Thus the pattern of conquest and settlement, the time-scale over which it occurred, and broadly, its impact upon Britain, needs to be covered. One must resist getting drawn into too much detail at this stage otherwise the topic could easily consume all the national curriculum time set aside for history.

Next you must choose to deal with one of the invaders in greater depth. For teachers who teach the same age group the same topic repeatedly, this is a blessing because, in most cases, it means that you do not repeat a topic more than once every three years.

The choices and the statutory requirements relating to them, are given below with the non-statutory examples removed. For these you should refer to the national curriculum document for history (p 6).

Choose for study in depth, either:

a **Romans**
- the Roman conquest and its impact on Britain
- everyday life
- the legacy of Roman rule

or:

b **Anglo-Saxons**
- the arrival and settlement of the Anglo-Saxons and their
- impact on Britain
- everyday life
- the legacy of settlement

or:

c **Vikings**

- Viking raids and settlement and their impact on Great Britain
- everyday life
- the legacy of settlement.

With the exemplary material removed, the identical pattern of treatment becomes clear. Also, equally clearly, one can see that the prescription leaves enormous scope for the selection of subject matter, variations in emphasis and a range of teaching styles.

Teaching the Key Elements and using this book

The photocopiable material and activities contained within this book are not intended to provide comprehensive coverage for this trinity of topics. It is not possible, for example, in a single sheet, to develop the complex narrative, which is required to unravel the sequence of events, which mark the conversion of the invaders from one side to the other of the heathen-Christian divide. For story and descriptive narrative you must, generally, look elsewhere. However, what this sort of material can do very well is to provide reinforcement to class teaching and in particular to help you to focus on and reinforce the skills taught through the Key Elements.

The Key Elements are rightly regarded as the backbone of the history curriculum, encapsulating, as they do, the core of the subject and much of what was previously set down under several attainment targets.

Many of the photocopiables are based upon evidence, so children will be getting to grips with Key Element 4. Indeed many of the activities are simply ways of making children look closely at evidence, to interrogate it and to draw conclusions from it. The Key Elements, to which the photocopiable sheets relate are:

1 **Chronology:** Everything concerned with placing events in time.

2 **Historical Knowledge and Understanding:** Facts, but also understanding them; reasons, causes and change.

3 **Interpretations:** How the past is presented and explained.

4 **Historical Enquiry:** Evidence, in all its forms, and its interrogation.

5 **Organisation and Communication:** Making public historical knowledge coherently in a variety of ways.

The national curriculum makes it quite clear that you are not expected to teach every Key Element in every historical topic so you can choose your material accordingly. We suggest that some very simple objectives be held in mind from the start, for example that, by the end of this topic children should:

- know something about the period (key events, personalities, what life was like then);
- have interrogated evidence from the period (photographs, objects or text);
- be able to make public their knowledge (in writing, speech or other form).

General teaching ideas

Chronology is important if the period is to be understood properly (see pages 46 and 85). A temporal framework needs to be established in the children's minds, not only of how the period relates to other periods studied, but also the relationship of events, within the period, to each other.

A sense of place is particularly important in this topic, which deals with the movement of people across Europe. Use a large wall map as a constant reference point just as you would use a time line. Mark routes, battles and events on it.

Key in, wherever possible, to the children's **own experiences**. Arguably no topic in the history national curriculum is more appropriate to our society, which is rich in immigrants and settlers from across the globe. Moreover, every locality in Britain has some links, through place-name or historic site, with one, if not all, of the waves of invaders and settlers dealt with in this study unit.

Try establishing a strong feel of the period through the use of all the senses. By using the colours, sounds, tastes and even smells of the period, one can create a memorable learning experience. Start with well-organised resources to encourage not only 'book' learning, but also learning through doing, for example, tasting Roman food, making deductions from a piece of evidence or trying out simple crafts. One does not need a vast array of resources, but the ability to see their potential for quality investigative work is important.

Set up a class museum. Get the children to appoint curators and advertisers and museum guides. Inspiration may be gained from a visit to a real museum (Jorvik and Corinium are two splendid examples). Focus on the interactive aspect of museum presentation. Schools have set up looms for weaving, built 'real' kilns and made pottery in period styles. Attention to detail pays dividends, for example, adding the smell of beeswax, the sounds of period music or the flickering light of an oil lamp.

Some schools have successfully used the school grounds for history projects by building outdoor kilns, Saxon huts and even a Roman hypocaust. Daily life, with its routine tasks of eating, sleeping, washing, cooking and cleaning can often be practised experimentally. Many schools have successfully undertaken 'history through drama' days, with extensive role play and hands-on experience. Such an event might focus on a day in a Saxon monastery, with different groups of monks doing tasks such as writing with a quill pen, tending a garden, making herbal remedies or singing chants. Building a Roman road or wall could also work; a problem-solving exercise as much as anything else. Get the children involved in the planning. How did the Romans do it? A craft fair is another possibility, bringing together fletchers, potters, embroiderers, candle makers and leather workers.

Role play, research and creative writing are some of the outcomes of work based on 'A Day in the Life of a ...'. Any character from the period could be chosen: a Roman school boy; the owner of a villa; an Anglo-Saxon farmer's wife; or a Viking warrior. First, the children must find out about their chosen person: What clothes did they wear? What games did they play? and so on.

Whatever written or creative work is done, make sure that it is presented with care, and properly valued by children and teacher alike. Making knowledge public is important, not just for communication and display purposes but as a reinforcement of knowledge learned. Telling somebody something about what you have learned, is also a test of understanding. Use lovely Celtic borders or Roman tessellated designs for displays and decorating work.

Resources

Artefacts, reproductions and facsimiles for the classroom

There are some excellent resources on the market but they can be costly. Often the best are to be found in your immediate locality. (A local museum officer may well turn out to be your best resource!) Even such unlikely places as charity shops can yield inexpensive material that, with a little imagination, can be more useful than products purchased from commercial suppliers. For example: items made out of natural materials such as leather, wood, copper, horn or clay; hand-crafted objects such as turned pots, woven cloth and basket work; suitable artefacts like a candle clock, a spindle, and a pestle and mortar; scavenged items such as goose feathers or a pig's bladder (from a butcher), birch twigs and hazel nuts from the woods, and rushes from the riverside. The ideal is probably a compromise between a few commercially produced facsimiles and your own collection supplemented by loans from your local library or museum.

Charity shops sell cheap garments that can be made into suitable costumes for role play. Make sure that only natural materials are selected and look for natural or dull colours. Thongs, brooches and leather sandals are useful accessories.

Retired people, especially grandparents, can be marvellous at making facsimiles given adequate picture references and instructions. Remember that classroom collections should be organised and catalogued.

Useful suppliers

Past Times shops in major cities and mail order. Past Times, Historical Collection Group plc, Witney, Oxfordshire OX8 6BH 01993 779444 (catalogue available)

History in Evidence: Unit 4, Holmefields Business Park, Park Road, Holmewood Chesterfield S42 5UY, Tel: 01246 856363 (catalogue available). This recently established company offers a substantial catalogue of historical artefacts for teachers such as an Anglo-Saxon coin set and a copy of King Athelwulf's ring.

Places to visit, including museums

Close is nearly always best as well as least expensive, when it comes to an educational visit. Unfortunately we cannot list all the places worth visiting or guarantee to include one close to you on our list, but the list does cover a range of significant and worthwhile sites. Small, but often very interesting, collections relating to this period are found in many small museums all over the country. They may not be very grand but they could be reasonably inexpensive to visit, and often provide excellent support to schools. A few of these are included in our list, which is arranged by geographical area:

Avon
Roman Baths Museum, Bath, Avon

Berkshire
Littlecote Roman Temple, Hungerford, Berkshire
Museum and Art Gallery, Reading, Berkshire
Museum, Wantage, Berkshire (Very small but has a specially commissioned copy of the Alfred Jewel itself a valuable antique.)

Dorset
Dorset County Museum, Dorchester, Dorset

Essex
Castle Museum, Colchester, Essex

Gloucestershire
Chedworth Villa, Chedworth, Gloucestershire
Corinium Museum, Park Street, Cirencester, Gloucestershire, GL7 2BX

Hampshire
City Museum, Winchester, Hampshire

Hertfordshire
Verulanium Museum, St Albans, Hertfordshire

Leicestershire
Jewry Wall Museum, Leicester

London
British Museum, Great Russell Street, London, WC1B 3DG (Tel: 0171 636 1555/6/7/8). Contains Sutton Hoo treasures, many Roman mosaics and the Anglo-Saxon Chronicle. Museum of London, 150 London Wall, London EC2Y 5HN

Kent
Lullingstone Villa, Lullingstone, Kent

Northumberland
Hadrian's Wall, Roman Army Museum (Hadrian's Wall World Heritage Site), Carvoran, Green Head, Northumberland
Vindolanda, The Vindolanda Trust, Chesterholm Museum, Bardon Mill, Hexham, Northumberland

Oxfordshire
Ashmolean Museum, Oxford. Holds the Alfred Jewel and that from Minster Lovell in its collection.

Scotland
Trimontium Exhibition, Ormiston Institute, The Square, Melrose, Roxburghshire

Somerset
South Cadbury Saxon Fort, Somerset

Suffolk
West Stow Anglo-Saxon Village, Icklingham Road, West Stow, Bury St Edmonds, Suffolk, IP28 6HG (Tel: 01284 728718) (Excellent reconstruction. West Stow also sells useful teaching materials, slides and books.)

Sussex
Fishbourne Roman Palace, Fishbourne Sussex
Roman Villa, Bignor, Sussex

Tyne and Wear
Arbeia Roman Fort, South Shields, Tyne and Wear
'Bede's World' Church Bank, Jarrow, Tyne and Wear, NE32 3DY (Tel: 0191 4892106). A new inter-active museum plus an Anglo-Saxon farm, open all the year.

Wales
Caerleon (Isca), near Newport, Gwent. Baths, amphitheatre and Legionary museum.

Wiltshire
Devizes Museum, 14 Long Street Devizes, Wiltshire 01380 727369

Yorkshire
Jorvik Viking Centre, Coppergate, York, YO1 1NT (Tel: 01904 643211)
Museum of Transport and Archaeology, Hull, Humberside
York, Roman and Viking sites, museums and collections.

General histories of the period and teachers' books

Morgan, Kenneth O, (ed), *The Oxford History of Britain*, Oxford, Oxford University Press, 1988, 0 19 285202 7

Shire Archaeology, Cromwell House, Church Street, Princes Risborough, HP17 9AJ. Shire produce a number of small handbooks, more than 12 covering this period, that contain a great deal of detailed expert information. For example:

Breeze, David J, *Roman Forts in Britain*, Shire, 1994, 0 85263 654 7

McWhirr, Alan, *Roman Crafts and Industries*, Shire, 1988, 0 85263 594 X

Anglo-Danish Viking Project, *Vikings in England*, 11 New Quebec Street, London W1H 7DD, 1981, 0 950743 20 8

Backhouse, Janet, *The Lindisfarne Gospels*, Phaidon, 1987, 0 7148 2461 5

Bradley, S A J, (trans), *Anglo-Saxon Poetry*, Dent, 1982, 0 460 11794 7

Campbell, James, (ed),*The Anglo-Saxons*, Penguin, 1991, 0 14 014395 5

Evans, Angela Care, *The Sutton Hoo Ship Burial*, British Museum Publications, 1989, 0 7141 0575 9

Garmonsway, G N, (trans), *The Anglo-Saxon Chronicle*, Dent, 1986, 0 460 87038 6

Grant, John, *An Introduction to Viking Mythology*, The Apple Press, 1990, 1 85076 225 2

Griffiths, Bill, (trans), *The Battle of Maldon*, Anglo-Saxon Books, 1991, 0 9516209 0 8. Contains a reconstruction of the source text.

Magnusson, Magnus and Palsson, Hermann, (trans), *Njal's Saga*, Penguin Classics, 1960, 0 14 044103 4

Potter, T W, *Roman Britain*, British Museum, 1990, 0 7141 2023 5

Sherley-Price, Leo, (trans), *Ecclesiastical History of the English People: Bede*, Penguin Classics, 1990, 0 14 044565 X

Wood, Michael, *In Search of the Dark Ages*, Penguin/BBC, 1994, 0 14 023884 0

English Heritage has produced an excellent series of teachers' guides (*Education on Site*) covering aspects of teaching the subject; a number of which provide useful help on this topic.
For example:

Durbin, Gail, Morris, Susan and Wilkinson, Sue, *Learning From Objects*, English Heritage, 1990, 1 85074 359 6

Mills, A D, *Dictionary of English Place-names*, Oxford, Oxford University Press, 1993, 0 19 283131 3

Children's books and classroom resources

Because the national curriculum lays down the history topics that must be taught, publishers have felt confident, for the first time for thirty years, that they could produce commercially viable pupils' books. More colourful and more interactive than earlier generations of textbooks, they also place a heavy emphasis on historical skills as well as historical knowledge. Increasingly teachers are using group and class sets as a core resource in the classroom. Of the many publishers producing such material, the most reliable and most comprehensive coverage of this topic (not only pupil books but teachers' notes and other support material) is provided by Ginn, Longman and, of course, Collins. Where known, the most recent print date has been given.

Collins Primary History:

Honnywill, Jill, *The Romans* (pupil book), Collins, 1991, 0 00 315450 5

Honnywill, Jill, *Anglo-Saxons and Vikings*, (pupil book), Collins, 1991, 0 00 313819 4

Honnywill, Jill, *Invaders: Romans, Anglo-Saxons and Vikings*, (teacher's guide), Collins, 1991, 0 00 313808 9

Noble, Paul, *The Romans Resource Pack*, (cards, charts, teacher's notes and photocopiables), Collins, 1991, 0 00 313797 X

Noble, Paul, *Anglo-Saxons and Vikings Resource Pack*, Collins, 1991, 0 00 315459 9

The range of children's reference books available on the Romans, Saxons and Vikings is substantial. A cross-section of more recently published books is listed. Some earlier publications are excellent, but might be difficult to obtain.

Baxter, Nicola, *Invaders and Settlers: Craft Topics*, Watts Group, 1994, 0 7496 1523 0

Blyth, Joan, *King Alfred, The Saxon Leader*, Chambers, 1977, 0 550 75514 4

Caselli, Giovanni, *A Viking Settler*, Macdonald, 1986, 0 356 11369 8

Clare, John D, *I Was There: Roman Empire*, Bodley Head, 1992, 0 370 31747 5

Clare, John D and Tweddle, Dominic, *I Was There: Vikings*, The Bodley Head, 1991, 0 370 31680 0

Ganeri, Anita, *Focus on the Vikings*, Franklin Watts, 1992, 0 7496 1018 2

James, Simon, *Ancient Rome*, (Eyewitness Guides), Dorling Kindersley/British Museum, 1990, 0 86318 445 6

Jarvie, Frances, *The Romans in Scotland*, National Museums of Scotland/HMSO, 1994, 0 11 494277 3

Loverance, Rowena, *The Anglo-Saxons*, BBC Fact Finders, BBC Educational Publishing, 1992, 0 563 35001 6

MacDonald, Fiona, *Vikings*, Oxford University Press, 1992, 0 19 910047 0

Margeson, Susan M, *Vikings* (Eyewitness Guides), Dorling Kindersley/British Museum 1994, 0 7513 6022 8

Martell, Hazel Mary, *What do we know about the Celts?*, Simon and Schuster Young Books, 1993, 0 7500 1245 5

Millard, Anne, *Eric the Red: The Vikings sail the Atlantic*, Evans, 1993, 0 237 51265 3

Museum of London, *Roman Gallery Resource Pack*, 150 London Wall, London EC2Y 5HN, 1993, 0 904818 45 4

Pearson, Anne, *The Vikings*, Hamlyn 1993, 0 600 57983 2. Contains some illustrations as 'see-through' transparencies.

Sharman, Margaret, *Anglo-Saxons*, Evans, 1995, 0 237 51456 7

Triggs, Tony, *Saxon Invaders and Settlers*, Wayland 1992, 0 7502 1356 6

Triggs, Tony, *Viking Invaders and Settlers*, Wayland 1992, 0 7502 1353 1

Williams, Brenda, *Roman Britain*, Hamlyn 1994, 0 600 58086 5

Wilson, David M, *The Vikings* (Activity Book), British Museum Press, 1993, 0 7141 0549 X

Wright, Rachel, *Vikings*, Franklin Watts, 1992

Computer programmes

The software prices are for Acorn computers, but some of the software can be bought in other formats (IBM and Nimbus). Where applicable the single user price has been given, otherwise it is the site licence price. You are advised to check with a good supplier, for example, AVP Educational Software, School Hill Centre, Chepstow, Gwent. Tel: 01291 625439. Your Information Technology (IT) adviser should also have full details on compatibility and availability.

Arcventure I: The Romans, Sherston, Acorn. This is an archaeological dig simulation.

Arcventure III: The Vikings, Sherston, Acorn. Jorvik dig.

Hedeby, Appian Way, Acorn. Based on the Viking town, includes support material.

Nag Burn, Appian Way, Acorn. Exploration of the Roman Wall and hence Roman military life.

The Roman Conquest of Britain, English Heritage.

Saxon Life, Oak Solutions, Acorn. Plots the course of the Saxon invasion extensive use of maps.

The Saxons, Garland, Acorn. Simulation for 8 year olds and over.

Viking England, Fernleaf, BBC B and Master. Story of Viking settlers from voyage to settlement.

Viking Invaders, Oak Solutions, Acorn. Genesis application includes photocopiables.

The Viking World, Anglia Television, Acorn. Draws on world-wide data in co-operation with the York Archaeological Trust.

Zig Zag: The Anglo-Saxons, Longman Logotron, Acorn. Focus on social life.

Zig Zag: The Romans, Longman Logotron, Acorn. Shows work on a Roman villa.

CD-ROM

Anglo-Saxons, Research Machines, IBM CD-ROM. Based on British Museum resources.

Radio and television

The Anglo-Saxons, BBC Zig Zag programmes; available as a video. CASE Television. Six part series covering Sutton Hoo, Bede, Beowulf and Alfred and the coming of the Vikings.

Consult the annually produced programme schedule of school broadcasts produced both by the BBC and Channel 4.

Posters, maps and charts

Most of the larger museums sell some excellent visual material especially slides, for example, Jorvik, The British Museum and West Stow Anglo-Saxon Village.

Ordnance Survey, in conjunction with city Archaeological Trusts and the Royal Commission on Historical Monuments (RCHM), has produced a series of historical maps as noted below:

Hadrian's Wall, 1:50 000 scale (2 cm to 1 km or 1.25 ins to 1 mile) and 1:25 000 scale (4 cm to 1 m or 2.5 ins to 1 mile), 0 31929018 2

Londinium (Roman London), 1:2500 scale (1 cm to 25 m or 25 ins to 1 mile), 0 319290 15 8, published in conjunction with the Museum of London.

Roman Britain, 1:625 000 scale (1 cm to 6.25 km or 1 in to 10 mile), 0 319290 27 1

Roman and Anglian York, 1:2500 scale (1 cm to 25 m or 25 ins to 1 mile), 0 319290 16 6, published in conjunction with York Archaeological Trust and RCHM

Roman and Medieval Bath, 1:2500 scale (1 cm to 25 m or 25 ins to 1 mile), published in conjunction with Bath Archaeological Trust and RCHM

Roman and Medieval Canterbury, 1:2500 scale (1 cm to 25 m or 25 ins to 1 mile), published in conjunction with the Canterbury Archaeological Trust and RCHM

Viking and Medieval York, 1:2500 scale (1 cm to 25 m or 25 ins to 1 mile), published in conjunction with York Archaeological Trust and RCHM

Pictorial Charts Educational Trust (PCET, 27 Kirchen Road, London W13 OUD Tel: 0181 567 9206), is the major supplier of educational charts for schools. They usually conform to a busy open-book style and are packed with information.

Invaders and Settlers , (H104), Frieze in three strips

Roman Britain: Home Life, (E101), Chart, 700x1000mm

Roman Britain: Invasion and Conquest, (E100), Chart, 700x1000mm

The Anglo-Saxons (E214), Chart, 700x1000mm

The Vikings (E213), Chart, 700x1000mm

Videos and tapes

Vikings, ISBN 349948 BBC Video Plus, BBC Educational Publishing, PO Box 234, Wetherby, West Yorkshire, LS23 7EU. Three programmes in the Zig Zag series, plus Teacher's Notes, full colour topic book and a classroom wallchart.

Sounds of the Viking Age, Audio cassette. Also *Sounds of the Roman Age* in the same series. Available from the Viking Museum York or Archaeologia Musica, PO Box 92, Cambridge CB4 1PU.

Historical fiction and story books

Clarke, P, *Torolv the Fatherless*, Faber, 1991

Crossley-Holland, K, *Beowulf*, illustrated by Charles Keeping, OUP, 1991. A version of the Saxon poem especially written for children.

Crossley-Holland, K, *Green Blades Rising: the Anglo-Saxons*, Andre Deutsch, 1975

Crossley-Holland, K, *Faber Book of Northern Legends*, Faber, 1977

Crossley-Holland, K, *The Sea Stranger*, Heinemann, 1973

Gordon, J, *The Giant Under The Snow*, Puffin, 1971, 0 14 030507 6

Green, Roger Lancelyn, *Myths of the Norsemen*, Puffin Classics, 1994, 0 14 036738 1

Hodges, C Walter, *The Marsh King*, Puffin, 1976

Hodges, C Walter, *The Namesake: a story of King Alfred*, C Walter Hodges, Puffin, 1976. Companion to *The Marsh King*.

Jones, T, *The Saga of Erik the Viking*, Pavilion, 1983

Leeson, R, *Beyond the Dragon Prow*, London, Collins Lions, 1976

Rosemary Sutcliff is the doyen when it comes to writing about this period but most of her books might prove too difficult for all but the most able primary children. They can readily be adapted and read aloud to children.

Sutcliff, R, *Blood Feud*, Puffin, 1978, 0 14 03185 1

Sutcliff, R, *The Capricorn Bracelet*, Red Fox, 1990

Sutcliff, R, *Eagle's Honour*, includes *The Circlet of Oak Leaves* and *Eagle's Egg* (for younger readers) Red Fox, 1995, 0 09 935391 1

Sutcliff, R, *The Eagle of the Ninth*, Puffin Modern Classics with OUP, 1994, 0 14 036457 9

Sutcliff, R, *Frontier Wolf*, Puffin/OUP, 1984

Sutcliff, R, *The Lantern Bearers*, Puffin/OUP, 1981, 0 14 031222 6

Sutcliff, R, *The Silver Branch*, Puffin, 1985, 0 14 031221 8

Sutcliff, R, *Song for a Dark Queen*, Puffin, 1987

Synge, U, *Weland, Smith of the Gods*, Bodley Head, 1972, 0 370 01268 2

Trease, G, *Word to Caesar*, Macmillan & Co, 1955

Trease, G, *Mist over Athelney*, MacMillan, 1958

Treece, Henry, *Legions of the Eagle*, Bodley Head, 1972, 0 370 00920 7

Treece, Henry, *Horned Helmet*, Hodder & Stoughton, 1986

Treece, Henry, *The Viking Saga* (trilogy), Puffin 1985, 0 14 031791 0

Treece, Henry, *Swords from the North*, Puffin, 1978

Trevor, M, *Merlin's Ring*

Useful addresses

There are courses run by experts in the crafts and skills of the Anglo-Saxons. Contact: The Longship Trading Company Ltd, 24 Dunloe Avenue, London, N17 6LA

Ermine Street Guard, c/o Oakland Farm, Dog Lane, Crickley Hill, Witcombe, Gloucester

Regia Anglorum, J K Siddorn, 9, Durleigh Close, Headley Park, Bristol, BS13 7NQ, Tel: 01272 646818. This group provides an interactive seminar for children lasting half a day, on the Saxons and/or Vikings. A wide range of artefacts and reproductions are used.

Cross-Curricular Links

Design and Technology

Test boat models: Roman and Viking

Roman technology: balusters, arches, groma

Wind propulsion experiments

Design and build waterwheels, arches

Houses:heating, lighting, plumbing and building techniques

Qualities of common materials used for tools

Science

Crop rotation and cultivation

Deforestation

Food and cooking in this period

PE and Dance

Create dances, for example, a dance to the Roman god Flora (hoops, petals and garlands)

Devise a fertility rite

Placate the gods

Art and Craft

Use Roman, Celtic, Saxon and Viking designs for inspiration

Model making: Viking boats, villas, tessellations

Rediscover early crafts: leatherwork, pottery, metalwork

Costume making: sandals, jewellery, tunics

Wax writing tablets

Fabric printing

Spinning weaving and dyeing

Coil pot making

Geography

Follow the invasion routes

Selection of sites for settlement

Use of land resources by settlers

Environmental effect of invasion and settlement

Plot the routes of Roman roads and defence posts

Britain from 54 BC to 1066

Music

Study instruments from pictorial evidence

Listen to re-creations of period music

Make replica instruments

Compose suitable music to accompany story-telling and drama

English

Myths and legends

Write riddles

Tell stories and sagas, including sequencing a narrative

Role play: create a Roman market in school

Writing and printing developments

Words: the legacy of the age in place-names and vocabulary

Keep a chronicle

Creative and descriptive writing:Letter from a soldier on Hadrian's Wall, Monk describing an attack on his monastery or similar

Mathematics

Surveying/measuring on site:Villa, Saxon church

Scale models

Investigating 'barter'

Roman numerals; try arithmetical calculations

Tessellations and regular polygons: Roman mosaics

Surveying using a 'groma'

Calculations with an abacus

Religious Education

Cultural and religious conflict

Missionaries and the spread of Christianity

Nature of different beliefs: gods and goddesses

Early Christian religious books:Lindisfarne Gospels

Saints

Visit Saxon church

Teacher's Time Line

54 BC	Caesar invades Britain: Cassivellaunus pays tribute
44 BC	Caesar murdered
AD 43	Roman conquest of Britain, Caractacus defeated
60	Boudica's revolt
84	Battle of *Mons Graupius* Celts defeated in Scotland
100	Greatest extent of Roman control in Britain
180	Retreat to Hadrian's Wall
360	Picts and Scots cross Hadrian's Wall and invade Roman Britain
383	Roman Legions begin to evacuate Britain
410	Alaric sacks Rome; Legions leave Britain to defend Rome
429	Saxons, Jutes and Angles push Picts and Scots out of southern Britain
436	Last Roman troops leave Britain
c 450	Kent and East Anglia settled by the Saxons
563	St Columba establishes the Iona community
577	Battle of Dyrham (nr Bath), Welsh defeated by West Saxons
597	King Ethelbert of Kent converted to Christianity by St Augustine
625	Sutton Hoo burial took place
635	Lindisfarne founded by Aidan
664	Synod of Whitby decides to follow the Roman rather than the Celtic Christian tradition
731	Bede's History is written
760	Offa's dyke built between England and Wales
793	Lindisfarne sacked by Viking raiders
806	Iona monastery sacked by Vikings
815	West Saxons defeat the West Welsh (Britons) who retreat into Cornwall
849	Birth of Alfred the Great (d. 899)
866	Danes establish kingdom of York
871	Alfred becomes King
878	Alfred makes a treaty with the Danish King Guthrum
954	Defeat and death of Eric Bloodaxe
991	Vikings defeat Saxons at the Battle of Maldon
1002	King Ethelred pays Danegeld of 24,000 pounds (1007, 36,000 pounds)
1016	King Cnut is king of England and Denmark
1046	King Edward the Confessor becomes king
1066	Normans (originally Vikings who settled in northern France) conquer England

The Romans

About four hundred years before the Roman conquest, traders from the Mediterranean had contact with these islands. Caesar came saw, but did not conquer, in 55 and again in 54BC. Later, after Caesar's death, plans to annexe Britain were made. Britain was rich in minerals, foodstuffs and people, but successful conquest was a valuable goal in itself to emperors and generals keen to prove their worth.

Eventually the Emperor Claudius and expedition commander, Aulus Plautius, invaded with an army of 40,000 in AD43. Britain was one of the last colonial acquisitions of the Empire.

At that time, Britain belonged to the Celts, a racial group widespread across Europe. The name Celt, however, covers a number of quite diverse tribes. The Belgae, Atrebates, Catuvellauni, Iceni, Durotriges, Regni and the numerous Brigantes of the north are, perhaps, the best known. The earliest Celtic civilisation existed in Austria around 750BC, but by AD74 all Celtic land in central Europe was controlled by the Romans.

Four legions soon subdued the Celts and Claudius himself led the triumphal Roman army into a Celtic capital near to modern Colchester. Capitals and strong points were captured one by one and a network of forts and roads established. Legionary and auxiliary soldiers garrisoned the land. A governor was appointed to run the province.

Britain was not subjugated in one sweep and there were set-backs. After Boudica's daughters were raped in AD60 and oppressive taxes imposed on Boudica's people, the Iceni and Trinovantes revolted and Colchester and London were sacked. With grim inevitability, 10,000 disciplined Romans put paid to the revolt and 80,000 Celts died. Boudica herself took poison.

From around AD70, forays were made northwards and York was established as a legionary fortress. By AD80 Roman armies had reached a line from the River Forth to the River Clyde. At the battle of *Mons Graupius* in AD84, Scotland was secured for the Emperor by an awesome defeat of the Celts, although the Highlands were never really subdued. It was the poverty of the area, which led to a gradual Roman retreat to the line of Hadrian's Wall. The Empire had over-reached itself and Scotland was not worth the effort required to retain it.

Throughout the Roman occupation, the population remained predominantly Celtic although it is clear that they became significantly Romanised. Many Romans took British wives and citizenship.

Not all Romans came from Rome or even Italy. Britain had around fifty governors between AD43 and AD213. Most were from Italy but Trajan and Hadrian came from Spain, Agricola from southern France and several, including Urbicus, came from North Africa.

Roman towns, with all their imposing grandeur, did not appear overnight in Britain. The wealth for public buildings had to be accumulated, and British towns never achieved the scale of Rome. Nevertheless the building of imposing temples on such sites as Colchester, must have had useful propaganda value, demonstrating the power and dominance of Rome.

In the later stages of Romano-Britain, the island flourished, perhaps because its island status insulated it from many of the conflicts on the continent. Wealthy villas became popular in the fourth century (some 600 plus sites are known). Britain became increasingly Christian, although no grand basilicas or churches were built, on the continental scale. Forts were constructed, mostly in the south and east, which was named the 'Saxon Shore'.

When, in AD367-8, Picts, Scots and Saxons combined to attack Roman Britain simultaneously, the commander of the Saxon Shore was killed. Only the intervention of a new army from Europe and a long campaign, restored Roman control. As troops were gradually recalled to defend Rome, the situation changed. The Saxon threat increased. Exactly when Britain and Rome parted company is not clear but in AD410 the Emperor Honorius wrote to the province telling towns 'to look to their own defence' and *Pax Romana* was all but gone.

Notes on the photocopiables

Map of the Roman Empire
(page 22)

The first Roman Emperor, Augustus, had a vision of the empire that was infinite, whereas later emperors had to come to terms with the idea of an empire with boundaries. That boundary separated the Roman civilised world from the barbarian. The northern British boundary to which the Romans retreated sometime after AD100, was the road line of the Stanegate, a little to the south of Hadrian's Wall.

Some surplus cereals and livestock were exported from Roman Britain but it was not a major producer of grain like Sicily or Egypt nor did it produce oil and wine in the huge quantities that came from Italy, Spain and north Africa. Britain became known for its woollen rugs and for a heavy type of duffle coat. The extraction of minerals – gold, silver, copper, tin, iron and lead – was closely controlled by the Roman authorities and was clearly important.

Slaves were a key stratum of society. The position of Roman slaves varied enormously. Many held important posts, some were able to gain their freedom. Slaves were taken in all the conquered territories.

- Explore the notion of empire so that the children understand what it is. Look at the words emperor, imperial, imperialism. How many empires can the children find out about? (Be aware of some of the children's links with the former British Empire.)

- Compare the produce traded by the empire with the produce of the comparable area of the modern world. Get the children to explore the shelves of a supermarket (or their own larders) for produce from the countries on the map. Collect product labels from these countries.

- Design labels for the Roman products mentioned.

Roman Britain (page 23)

It required a Roman garrison to keep Britain subdued and even then inept and cruel government could trigger revolts (like the Boudica led one in AD60) which were costly and difficult to put down. Nevertheless Britain enjoyed considerable security under Rome and the legions were mainly employed in holding the frontiers against attack from outside.

An Ordnance Survey map (Scale 1:50 000) will reveal any Roman sites in your area although special OS maps are produced of Roman Britain. Roman roads joined the major towns, legionary fortresses and Coloniae (colonies of retired soldiers). At one time, the Fosse Way, which runs from Lincoln to Exeter, marked a temporary early boundary of Roman control.

- Produce a 'Roman' map of your locality. Try to create a picture of the area in Roman times.

- Investigate how the Romans built their roads. You may be able to construct a sample section in the school grounds.

- Visit a good Roman site.

Celtic Warriors (page 24)

Although the Celts did enjoy some successes against the Romans, notably Boudica's defeat of the 9th legion north of Colchester in an ambush, they were few and far between. They did not lack courage or military qualities – they were widely employed as mercenaries – but all over Europe the Romans defeated them. At *Mons Graupius* near Aberdeen, 11,000 Romans defeated 30,000 Celts. The 10,000 legionaries in reserve did not fight at all and only 400 Romans died. Boudica's revolt was put down by a considerably inferior Roman force numerically. The reasons were superior Roman discipline and training, tactics and weaponry.

The densely-packed masses of Celts, with little or no armour, were first decimated by thousands of heavy javelins thrown at short range, then the legions moved forwards in tight formation behind their large shields. Under these confined conditions the long Celtic swords were no match for the stabbing thrusts of the Roman troops. Highly mobile cavalry worked around the enemies flanks causing panic. Most of the slaughter took place as the Celtic armies broke and fled.

- Equip a Celtic warrior. This could be a large piece of artwork or a matter of dressing a volunteer. Alongside, for comparison, display a Roman soldier.

- Tell the story of a battle of Celts against Romans. (Use historical fiction – see *Resources*.)

Celtic War Trumpet (page 25)

Contemporary (admittedly biased) sources describe the Celts as being variously 'boastful, threatening, high-spirited, war-like and superstitious'. The noise and sight of a Celtic army must have been highly intimidating but the Roman commander against Boudica told his men to 'ignore the racket made by these savages'. Part of the 'racket' was made by the carnyx.

The boar was the most sacred creature to the Celts, probably because they admired its ferocity. It is not surprising that the head of the battle trumpet was shaped like a wild boar. When blown, the carnyx is thought to have reproduce the scream of a wild pig.

- Experiment with the mouthpiece (only) of a recorder to reproduce suitable pig screaming sounds. Try out other instruments and methods. (Note that, as with all wind instruments, the sound produced depends on the way it is blown.)

- Make a recording of a 'radio' reporter at the battle of *Mons Graupius*. Describe the battle and hear the sounds!

In the Roman Army (page 26)

These fascinating insights into life in the Roman army, are provided by the late fourth century author Flavius Renatus Vegetius. His treatise *De Re Militari* (A Book about Military Affairs) describes in detail how the Roman Military system worked. The measurements quoted have been converted to modern imperial and metric dimensions.

- As a class, or in groups, make a Roman Army Training Manual. This could be a large wall book illustrated to match the text. Make sure the children stick to the evidence!

- Construct a Roman army assault course based on Vegetius's book. This could be a fun challenge with a difference for Sports Day. Keep a wary eye on potential safety hazards.

A Roman Camp (page 27)

Flavius Josephus, who wrote *De Bello Judaico* (A History of the Jewish War) about the Jewish revolt against the Romans AD66-70, was himself a Jew. In the year AD63 he travelled to Rome and became a friend of Nero's second wife. He became convinced that the Roman military machine was invincible and tried to persuade his countrymen not to go to war against it. When war did break out, he became an officer in the Jewish army, was captured by the Romans and taken to Rome. He became friendly with three successive emperors and was eventually granted Roman citizenship. He died around AD100.

- More able children might enjoy doing some detective work on this text. Was the writer a Roman? Did he think the Roman army was a good army? How can you tell?

- Get children to highlight words that they are not sure of. Make an illustrated dictionary of these terms.

- Construct a class model using this evidence.

- Write an illustrated manual, 'Camping for Romans', based on this photocopiable. (It is probably best to divide this task among groups of children.)

Roman Soldiers (pages 28-29)

The key officer was the centurion in charge of a unit of 80 men. His second in command was called an optio. A signifier carried the wooden pole decorated with the battle honours of each 'century'. The standard bearer carried a flag with the legion's symbol on it.

Discipline was strict in the army with reduction in pay, extra duties or loss of rations used as standard punishment.The soldiers took it in turns to gather wood, find food and haul water. Each unit bore its share of the work. The men ate meals together. Nothing was done except by command. Trumpets signalled the hours for sleep, guard duty and waking.

Any serious offence was punished by death. Soldiers were not allowed to marry during military service but nevertheless they often had offspring and partners to support outside the barracks. Roman soldiers, particularly the auxiliaries, came from all over the empire. There is evidence in Britain of soldiers from Palmyra in Syria, Bejaia in Algeria and many from Germany. Celtic mercenaries were common.

- Use small replicated drawings to create a visual image of a century of soldiers.

- Using information from this and other sheets (pages 27, 28-29, 30-31) the children should have a reasonable idea of what life in the army was like. Get them to write a letter home from a posting in Britain. Choose a real place in the empire to which to write. (See page 22.)

A Roman Helmet/Roman Infantryman (pages 30-31)

Both of these sheets provide information on a Roman soldier's kit.

- Make an infantryman's full kit for display.

- Dress up in Roman kit. (Not a task to be taken on lightly but worth doing for a display, assembly or play. Get parental help but always remember to stick as closely as possible to the evidence.)

- Compare Roman kit with a modern infantryman's equipment. The local army recruiting office may help you with this. How much do both weigh?

Numeral Quiz (page 32)

For convenience the solution to the number crossword is given below. Note two ways of showing forty (40): XXXX and XL.

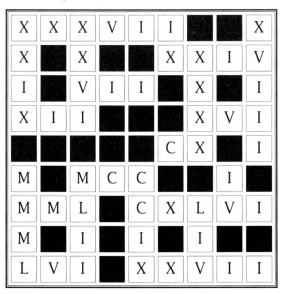

- Get children to look for Roman numerals around them. Inscriptions, memorials, plaques, book publication dates and, quite commonly for no reason that we can fathom, BBC programme production dates and Hollywood film release dates are good places to find Roman numerals being used.

- Try doing Roman arithmetic (the four rules). Work out ways of setting it down. What number (or placeholder) did the Romans lack?

Roman Villa (pages 33-34)

Villas ranged from working farms to small settlements to a rich man's estate. This sheet is based upon a wealthy Roman's estate.

- Continue the wordsearch with the aid of a dictionary and look for English words (around the house) which contain Roman roots, for example, culinary (*culina*), cubicle (*cubiculum*).

- Draw a plan of the villa from the drawing and the information given.

- Visit the site of a Roman villa. Get the children to sketch the villa *in situ* as it used to be.

Wax Writing Tablet (page 35)

You can take the easy way out and use plasticine or clay which will be fun, but not historically correct; neither will the children get an insight into a world of low technology. Any solutions to the problems encountered with the wax tablet will be real ones. Our drawings show the tablet being made by gluing the base and balsa wood for the frame, rather than cutting the wood and nailing on the frame, such as might be done with a technology kit. Whichever method you use for making the base, melting the beeswax will need careful supervision. We did it in an old saucepan, but it could be done in a microwave oven, using a non-metal container.

Roman writing (non-cursive) was designed that way to make it easy to write on the materials available. Paper was unknown in the west. The serifs are explained by the way stonemasons needed to make a first incision when incising letters in stone. The serifs survive, largely without function, other than elegance, in some modern typefaces – this one included.

But the handwriting used for daily communication was very different from the Roman capitals inscribed on tombstones. The Romans wrote on wax with a stylus (iron, bronze and ivory examples exist) or in ink on wooden tablets or papyrus rolls. Very little of this sort of writing has survived. Latin and Greek (in the eastern empire) were the languages written down. The Roman alphabet which we still use today, had 22 letters – I and J were treated as the same and U, V, W, and Y did not exist.

- The main ingredient of Roman ink was soot. Investigate ways of making ink from commonly found ingredients.

- The development of writing and printing (a thematic study from the pre-Dearing curriculum) makes a project in itself and is worth doing as a class (See Collins Resource Pack: *Writing and Printing*).

Mosaics (page 36)

From around 300 years before the birth of Christ, mosaic patterned floors are known to have existed, the earliest in Greece and Sicily. As Rome expanded it spread the art across the empire. Numerous examples survived in Britain up to the seventeenth century (over 1100) but many have since been destroyed by urban development and vandalism. Fine examples are displayed in the British Museum and at Roman sites and in Museum collections around the country. One of the finest is the recently restored 'Orpheus Mosaic' at Littlecote near Hungerford, Berkshire.

Tesserae is the name given to the small cubic tiles from which mosaics were made (hence tessellation). These were set in a lime mortar over a gravel foundation and grouted with a mixture of very fine mortar. Mosaics were used on pavements, floors and even walls as European basilicas testify, and were built up from a range of standard patterns. The tesserae were largely cut from stone. Red, white and blue are the dominant colours. Glass, brick, tiles, chalk, marble, sandstone, limestone and ironstone were some of the materials used.

- Bake your own clay tesserae in a kiln and make your own mosaic. Set in thistle plaster on a plywood base and

frame with a wooden beading ready for hanging.

- Investigate geometric shapes that will tessellate. (An investigation of polyominoes – especially pentominoes – fits well as a maths topic alongside this project.) More able children may be able to understand why some shapes tessellate and others do not (angles at the junctions of shapes must add up to 360 degrees).

Toga (page 37)

Togas were not casual wear. They perhaps best equate to the modern status of the suit. Short sleeveless tunics were daily attire but on formal occasions out came the heavy wrap-round toga, almost always in white. Only the emperor was allowed to wear purple (the most expensive dye). Any other citizen putting on purple was committing an act of treason. Trousers were regarded as effeminate.

- Pretend to be a fashion correspondent in a magazine and write a fashion review of toga on the catwalk.

- The best way to appreciate the toga is to make one and to try it on.

Drape the material over your left shoulder, so that it reaches your ankles. Hold it firm by tucking some material under your left arm. Ask a friend to wrap the rest round your body, under your right arm, and then up to your left shoulder. Secure it with a brooch.

Shops (page 38)

Shops were a feature of towns and their layout would not seem unfamiliar to us today. A 1950s grocer would display his wares outside under an awning and weigh and serve customers in the cramped interior across a counter – Roman shops were very similar. Most shops had living quarters above the shop, where the owner lived. The ones featured on this page are:
A: Clothes, B: Cutler, C: Butcher,
D: Pharmacy/Soapmaker, E: Fruit Seller

This 'For Sale' notice from Pompeii gives us the flavour of the time:

The Arrius Pollio Apartment Complex owned by Gnaeus Allius Nigidius Maius
FOR RENT from 1 July
street-front shops with counter space,

luxurious second-storey apartments, and a townhouse.
Prospective renters, please make arrangements with Primus, slave of Gnaeus Allius Nigidius Maius.

- Set up a Roman market in the school hall or playground. Make items to sell for school funds. (For example, wine [red grape juice], jewellery, pottery lamps, bunches of herbs, candles and leather goods.)

- Using a slab of clay as the base, build up and incise a plaque showing a Roman shop.

- Devise an advertisement for the sale of a Roman shop. List its advantages as selling points.

A Taste of Rome/Kitchen

(pages 39-40)

A Taste of Rome gives an indication of some of the basic foods consumed by the Romans in Britain. They also farmed oysters, snails and edible dormice. The latter survive as a protected species around Tring in Hertfordshire. Many foods for the wealthier Romans, such as wine and pomegranates, would have been imported.

Apicius, who lived in the early imperial period, wrote a cookery book which has provided considerable insights into eating for the wealthy. The book was published some three hundred years after his death, so he may not have been responsible for every recipe. Apicius places a great deal of emphasis on preserving foods and on making stale food palatable; skills that must have been essential in the days before refrigerators. Strong sauces were commonly used to mask natural flavours. *Liquamen* was the most common seasoning (a strong fish stock), and *silphium* was the most valued herb. It has been argued that the strong flavours were used to revive appetites that were flagging as a result of the intake of lead. This came from the widespread use of lead-lined pots. Another argument suggests that spices were expensive and hard to come by, therefore only the rich could afford the range of taste possibilities which they provided. Using alternative strong flavours was a cheap way of emulating the wealthy.

Basic kitchen equipment has not changed much. Saucepans and skillets, colanders and pastry cutters can be found in modern kitchens as well as in the ruins of Pompeii. Instead of food mixers and dish-washers the Romans had slaves. Most of the cooking was done over a raised hearth fired with charcoal. Cooking pots were placed on tripods or gridirons. A low oven was used for baking. The fire was raked out, then the pies or cakes placed in it. The entrance was sealed to keep in as much heat as possible. Keeping the pots clean was not easy, and the large quantities of broken pottery, found near Roman ovens, suggest that earthenware needed to be replaced constantly.

- Ask the questions on the sheet about modern cooking by way of comparison. Can you explain the differences?

- Do a stock-taking exercise in a modern kitchen (the school kitchen?) and compare.

- Some museums (Corinium in Cirencester for example) have recreated Roman kitchens and Roman herb gardens. It is worth visiting, if you can.

- Plant your own Roman herb garden.

Helping the Sick (page 41)

Painkillers as we know them did not exist, although alcohol was, no doubt, used to dull the pain. As in all pre-scientific times, the causes of disease were little understood so most treatments were inadequate or inappropriate and many were dangerous. Surgery was hazardous because of poor hygiene and no anaesthetics. Major and even minor fractures were either fatal or led to amputation. Appendicitis and compli-cations in childbirth that are dealt with routinely today, regularly proved to be fatal. Nevertheless, herbal remedies for common maladies were used with great effect, and the skill of surgeons in dealing with battle wounds, for example, was considerable. The medical instruments in the picture include: a rectal speculum, a bleeding cup, a hook, probes, spoon, forceps, scalpel and a box for drugs.

A wide range of herbal medicines was available. The Roman writer Pliny listed forty, whose main ingredient was mustard.

- Carry out a dictionary search for

English words with Latin roots (based on the selection given).

ambulare [to walk]

amputare [to cut off]

casus [fall]

doctus [skilled]

hospitium [guest house]

invalidus [weak]

medicus [doctor]

opera [work]

patiens [suffering]

Spot the Gods (page 42)

The Romans taste in gods was a catholic one. Not only did they have hundreds of gods, goddesses, demi-gods and spirits available for worship across the empire, they were usually quite happy to pick up a few local ones if they felt it might do them some good. Such a multi-god society could only really function if there was a climate of tolerance for other people's choice of gods. One of the reasons why the Christians fared so badly at the hands of the Romans was that the Judeo-Christian belief in one God excluded all others. It was (and is) a religion that did (and does) not allow the worship of other deities.

Egyptian gods were enjoyed by the Romans because they suggested and gave hope for an afterlife. Romans also believed it was possible to become a god, at least the emperors thought so. Many of them, after their deaths, were declared to be gods.

Religious practice was largely a matter of sacrifice and offering up prayers and promises. Religious offerings took place in temples or at shrines where the Romans believed the gods to be. A temple was literally 'the house of god'.

During the fourth century, Christianity began to replace the old gods as it spread throughout the Roman world. Eventually it became the religion of the emperors.

- Explore Roman connections with the life of Christ (RE) as given in the Bible. (Use reference books or a Bible concordance to help.)

- Find out about religions known to the children (multi-faith project).

- Be creative on the subject of Roman gods. Paint them (a giant classroom frieze is impressive), write poems about them or make clay models of them.

- Compile a class book of Roman gods including as much information as you can.

The answers to the sentences about the gods are as follows reading top left to bottom right:

1 VENUS	2 DIANA
3 MERCURY	4 JANUS
5 BACCHUS	6 JUPITER

How did they do that?
(page 43)

Roman technology was basic by our standards but very effective. Remarkable buildings, sophisticated plumbing, and astonishing feats of civil, not to say military, engineering bear witness to this fact.

The examples shown are:
a rope mechanism used for turning a heavy stone column during the process of carving and preparing it for erection;

a groma, which was a simple sighting device set at 90 degrees that was used to build straight roads and to make sure that roads intersected, accurately, at right angles.

- Make working models of this technology to understand how it actually worked.

- Investigate other Roman technical skills (building arches, constructing viaducts or hypocausts).

Country Life (page 44)

The range and variety of country activities taking place in and around this villa is considerable. The evidence is not entirely clear because of the ravages of time and because the photograph is clearly evidence at second hand. However, the lack of clarity is a virtue in one sense. By studying this picture, the children can appreciate how difficult a historian's job can be and that, acting as historians, they have to make judgements and come to conclusions based upon clues that are not always conclusive. Evidence is rarely complete and totally reliable. Provided that the children can make a good case for their observations on this picture, their opinion is as good as that of anyone else.

There are at least a dozen activities pictured here.

This tessellated scene comes from North Africa and can be viewed at the Bardo Museum, Tunis.

- Interrogate the scene. Who made it? Why was it made? What does it tell us about the people who made it? What is it? What is its value?

- Make a wall size reproduction of this scene. This could be done in sections as a painting or mosaic using coloured paper. (See the notes on mosaics for ideas about colours.) This could be annotated with descriptions of the activities pictured.

- Create then and now scenes of the individual activities. Research will be needed. What does a modern irrigation scheme look like? You could have an interesting debate about what constitutes comparable modern activities. (When do we hunt for food?)

Mystery Roman Objects Quiz (page 45)

The answers to the object quiz are:

1 Gold coins. These were part of a hoard buried in Kent in AD43 probably by a soldier in the invasion force. It represented, to a legionary, four years' salary.

2 Oil lamp. You can see the hole for the wick and for the oil in this small oil lamp.

3 Vine pruning knives.

4 Wooden writing tablet. The stylus would have been used to inscribe on the wax, which would have filled this folding Roman equivalent of a note book.

- Interrogate all of these items as evidence using a systematic method. You might devise a proforma for the children to use. First describe, then deal with function, likely provenance and worth. (For further guidance, see Country Life, page 44.)

- Try making reproductions of one of these items.

- Tell the story of one of these items. How did it come to be in a museum?

- Draw one of the objects from at least two different angles. How accurate will your drawings be? Alternatively, draw cross-sections of the objects as an archaeologist might do.

- Collect and display modern objects that correspond as closely as possible to the Roman ones and place them next to the pictures for comparison.

Roman Time Line (page 46)

It is helpful at some point to relate the Roman period visually to today as well as to other periods studied by the children. A class time line is useful for this purpose. Precise dating is not crucial; get the centuries right and the relative positions of periods correct. This is something the children should be encouraged to do themselves. An easily rearranged time line, using a string and pegs, velcro fasteners or clips is the best option. Make the time line pictorial not just a display of numbers and words. Try making a time line which covers a long period of time, that is several historical periods. It is even more interesting if you can use real objects, but copies will do.

Christmas is something all children will know about so use the opportunity to establish the idea of AD and BC and of year 1. (There is no year nought!) There are other Roman dates the children could add for themselves (murder of Caesar, sack of Rome, battle of *Mons Graupius* and so on). Encourage some research.

- Let the children make their own individual 'Invaders' time lines – it could be constructed as a long zig-zag.

Map of the Roman Empire

This map shows the Roman Empire 2,000 years ago.

- In what language are the names written?

- List as many modern names as you can, for example:
  AEGYPTUS = EGYPT

- Name the countries which gave Rome wine, slaves, cloth, corn and metals.

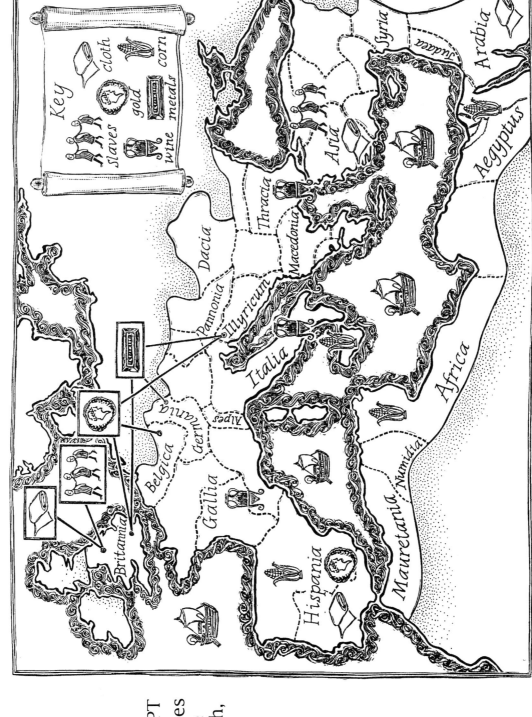

Key

cloth

gold

wine   metals   corn

slaves

Roman Britain

- What places did the roads join? Why?
- Which is the nearest Roman road to where you live?
- Which is your nearest Roman city?

Find out why most of the forts were in the north or in Wales.

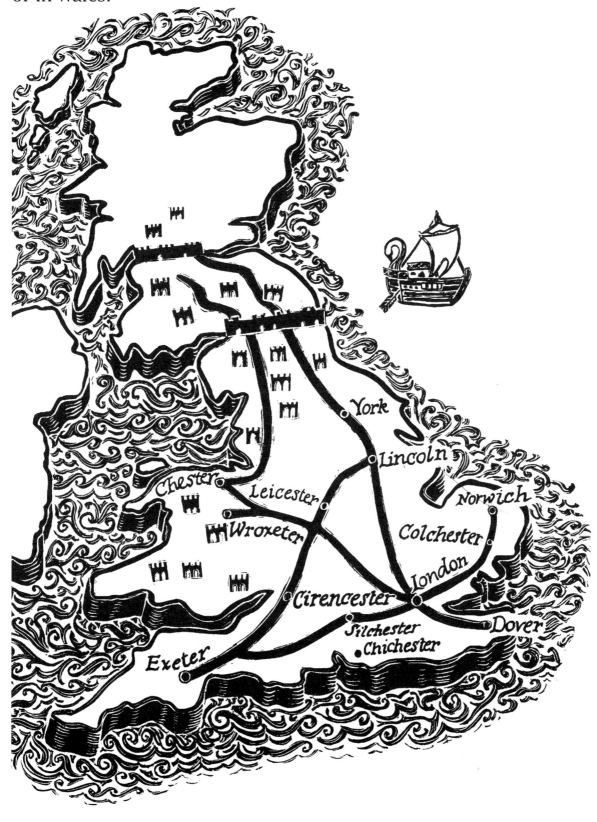

Celtic Warriors

The Romans conquered the Celts. Roman soldiers were well-equipped, trained and organised. The Celts hardly ever fought as an army. At one battle, north of Aberdeen in Scotland (*Mons Graupius*), 11,000 Romans overpowered 30,000 Celts. The 10,000 legionaries in reserve did not fight at all and only 400 Romans died.

• Why?

Some reasons are listed here. Write them in the correct circle.

Put the reasons which fit both the Romans and the Celtic warriors in the area between.

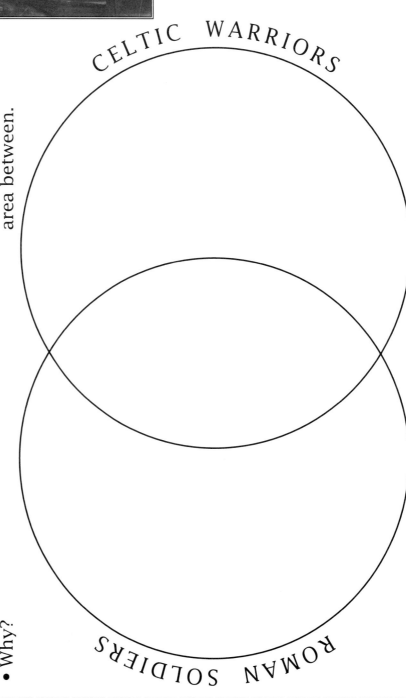

well disciplined
large, heavy iron swords
fast cavalry
slow battle chariots
short stabbing swords
brave fighters
small shields with magical designs
large rectangular shields
metal armour protection
little or no armour worn

CELTIC WARRIORS

ROMAN SOLDIERS

Celtic War Trumpet

As they went into battle, the Celts blew wild screams on their war trumpets. The instrument had no holes or valves and made a terrifying sound like a screaming pig. The head was shaped like a wild boar. It was called a CARNYX.

Frighten your classmates with a carnyx!

To make one you will need:

- a hollow tube for the trumpet
- card, glue and pins to make the head (you could shape one out of clay and cover it with papier-mache)
- large beads for eyes
- paint and varnish (Marvin medium or similar will do)

Try using the mouthpiece of an old recorder to make the screaming noise.

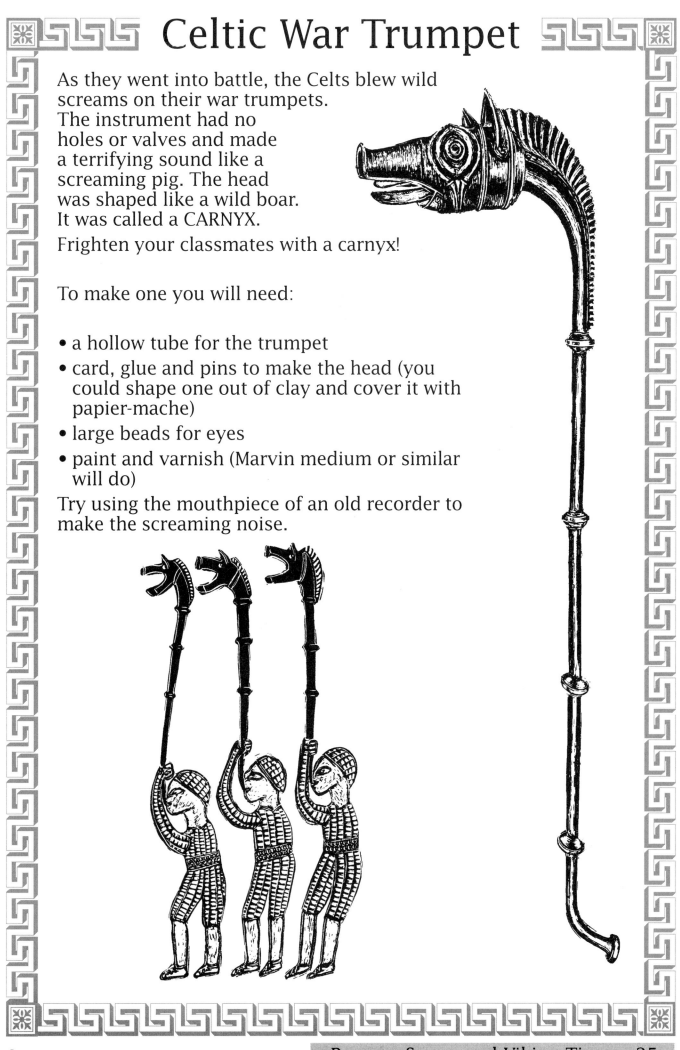

In the Roman Army

- Make a recruiting poster for the Roman Army. Use the information from these Roman documents.

TRAINING

RECRUITS must be taught the military pace. They must practise continuously marching quickly and in time. At full pace, 21 miles should be completed in five hours.

SOLDIERS must also be trained to jump so that they can leap ditches and other obstacles. Every recruit should learn how to swim, for rivers cannot always be crossed by bridges. An army is often forced to swim in order to follow the enemy or in order to retreat.

RECRUITS should train at the stakes with wooden swords and shields of double the normal weight not only in the morning but in the afternoon.

ALL soldiers constantly should practise vaulting on to horses. This should be done indoors on wooden horses in the winter.

THEY must frequently carry loads of up to 43 pounds (20kg), run with their armour and baggage and cut down trees.

VEGETIUS, *A Book about Military Affairs*

RECRUITS

RECRUITS have always been required to be of a minimum height. Only men 5 feet 10 inches (1.80 metres) or at least 5 feet 8 inches (1.75 metres) have been accepted for the cavalry or the first cohorts of the legions. But in those days more men wanted to join the army. Nowadays there is a shortage of recruits so it is necessary to take notice of a man's strength rather than his height.

VEGETIUS, *A Book about Military Affairs*

A Roman Camp

This was written when the Romans ruled the known world:

THE Romans are never caught unexpectedly by an attack of the enemy. Whatever land they invade, they do not do battle until they have made a camp.

If the ground is uneven it is levelled. A square camp site is measured out. It is divided into areas for tents. The outer wall has towers built at regular intervals. Between the towers they set up catapults and stone-throwing engines ready for firing. Four gates are then built; one on each side of the camp.

The camp is divided symmetrically into streets. In the middle one are tents for officers and at the very centre the general's headquarters.

Very soon a city, with a market place and an assembly area, appears. If necessary a ditch is dug outside the walls.

JOSEPHUS, *A History of the Jewish War*

- Draw a plan of a Roman camp using the written evidence. The picture will also help.
- Label all the details mentioned in the description.

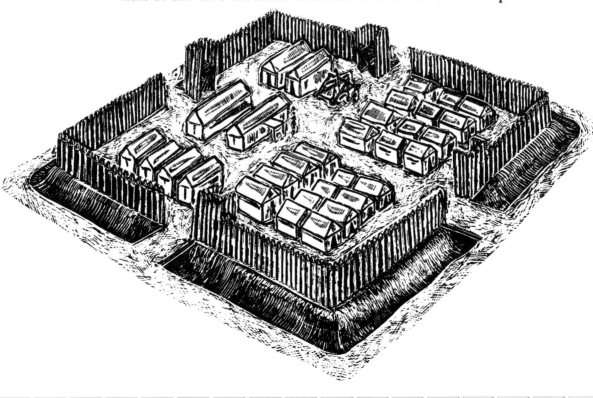

Roman Soldiers 1

- Cut out the soldiers and the descriptions separately.
- Match them correctly and stick them on to coloured paper.
- Who were the most important soldiers? • Can you place them in order of rank?

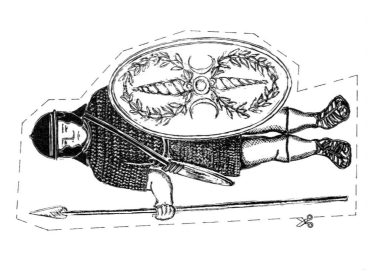

LEGIONARY SOLDIER

He wore armour plates and carried a shield and a long javelin. He was a Roman citizen.

STANDARD BEARER

Like the Signifier, he wore bearskin or lion skin on his head. On the standard bearer's flag was the symbol of the legion. The symbol of the 20th legion was a boar.

SIGNIFIER

Each company of men, under the charge of a centurion, had its own battle standard held by the signifier. The standard was a wooden pole to which battle honours were attached.

Roman Soldiers 2

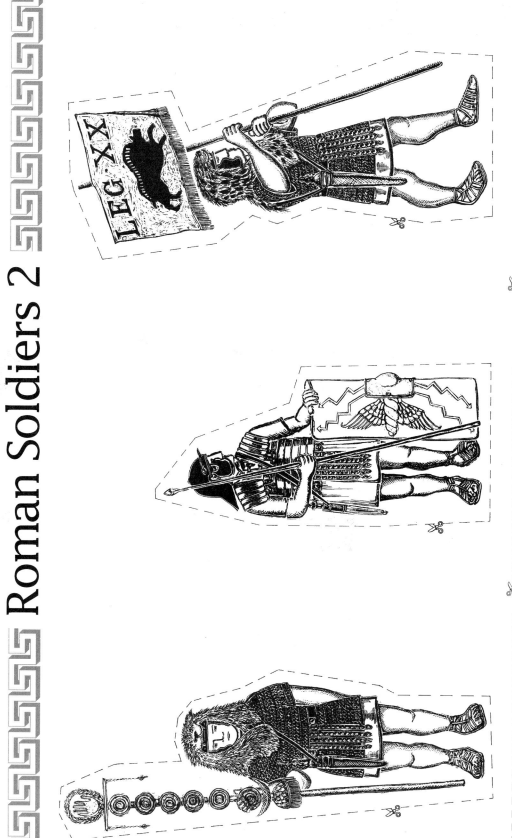

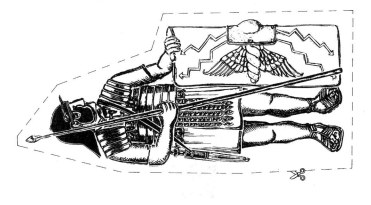

AUXILIARY

If he stayed in the army for 25 years the auxiliary was made a Roman citizen. He usually came from one of the lands that Rome had conquered. He wore a chain mail shirt.

HORN PLAYER

He played an instrument called the *cornu* and made the trumpet calls in camp and on the march so that the soldiers could act together.

CENTURION

He was an officer in charge of 80 men. He wore shinguards to protect his legs and a crest, on his helmet, ran from side to side, so that his men could see him in battle.

A Roman Helmet

Follow the instructions in the drawings to make a helmet. (You could use an old hat cut down to size for the main section.)

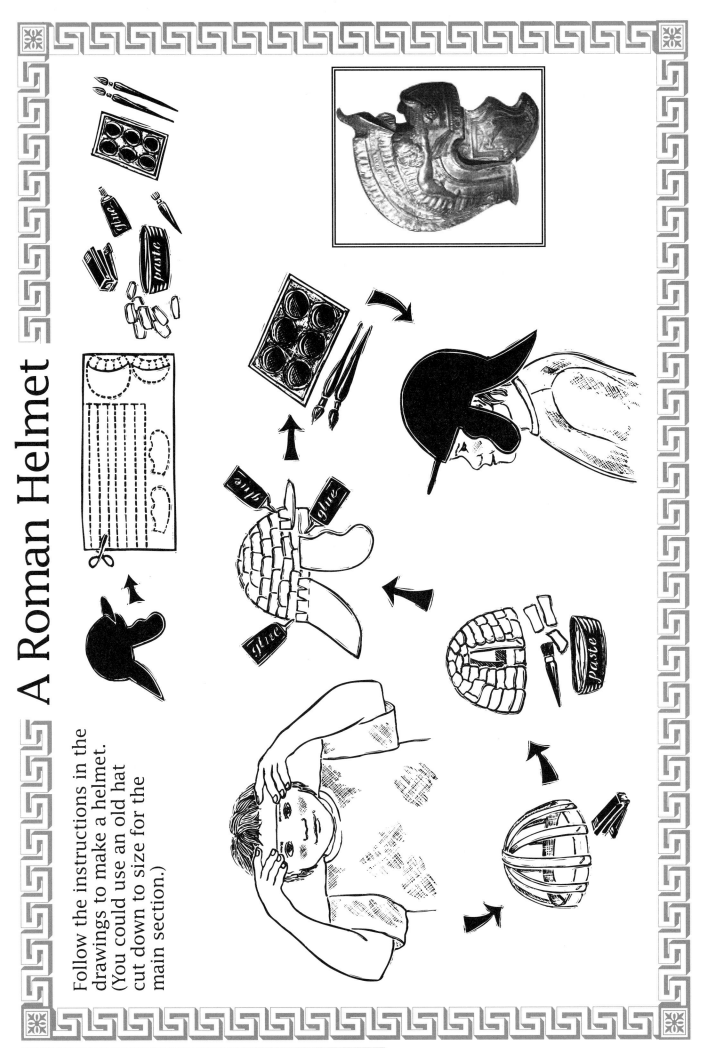

A Roman Infantryman

- Look at the picture of the infantryman carefully.
- What other name might we give the very short sword? (See the scroll below.)
- Add the equipment, described on the scroll below, to the soldier on this page.

The infantry are equipped with breastplates and helmets and carry a sword on both sides. The sword on the left is much longer than the one on the right side which is no longer than a span (about 4 inches or 10 cm) in length. They also carry a javelin and an oblong shield. The infantryman is very like a loaded pack mule for he also has a saw, a basket, a shovel and axe, as well as a scythe, a chain and three days' food rations.

JOSEPHUS,
A History of the Jewish War

Numeral Quiz

Clues: Across

1 37   5 24   7 7   8 12   9 16   10 110

12 .1200   15 .2050   16 ...146   18 56   19 27

Clues: Down

1 29

2 26

3 9

4 18

6 40

11 ..3050

12 ..1052

13 209

14 4

17 54

Roman numerals

I	1	VII	7	L	50
II	2	VIII	8	C	100
III	3	IX	9	D	500
IV	4	X	10	M	1000
V	5	XI	11	MM	2000
VI	6	XII	12		

- Write the year in Roman numerals.

Roman numerals are still used today.

How many miles is that?

Roman Villa 1

Find the Latin words the Romans used
to name the rooms and other parts of their villas.
They are in the word square.

CVBICVLVM
HORTVS
TRICLINIVM
POSTICVM
TABERNA
ANDRON
TABLINIVM
ATRIVM
CVLINA
ALA
IMPLVVIVM

H	O	R	T	U	S	T	V
A	T	I	O	P	T	R	I
M	A	N	V	O	A	I	N
I	B	E	C	L	B	C	T
A	L	A	T	A	E	L	I
M	I	B	L	M	R	I	A
A	N	D	R	O	N	N	T
C	I	O	C	N	A	I	M
I	U	V	U	A	M	U	U
K	M	L	B	R	Y	M	I
A	T	R	I	U	M	A	V
G	X	T	C	N	N	P	U
E	I	M	U	V	A	U	L
U	P	L	L	Y	S	A	P
B	T	R	U	C	P	I	M
O	N	U	M	I	S	U	I
M	U	C	I	T	S	O	P

bedroom
garden
dining room
back door
shop/inn
passage
living room
hall
kitchen
side room
rainwater basin

Roman Villa 2

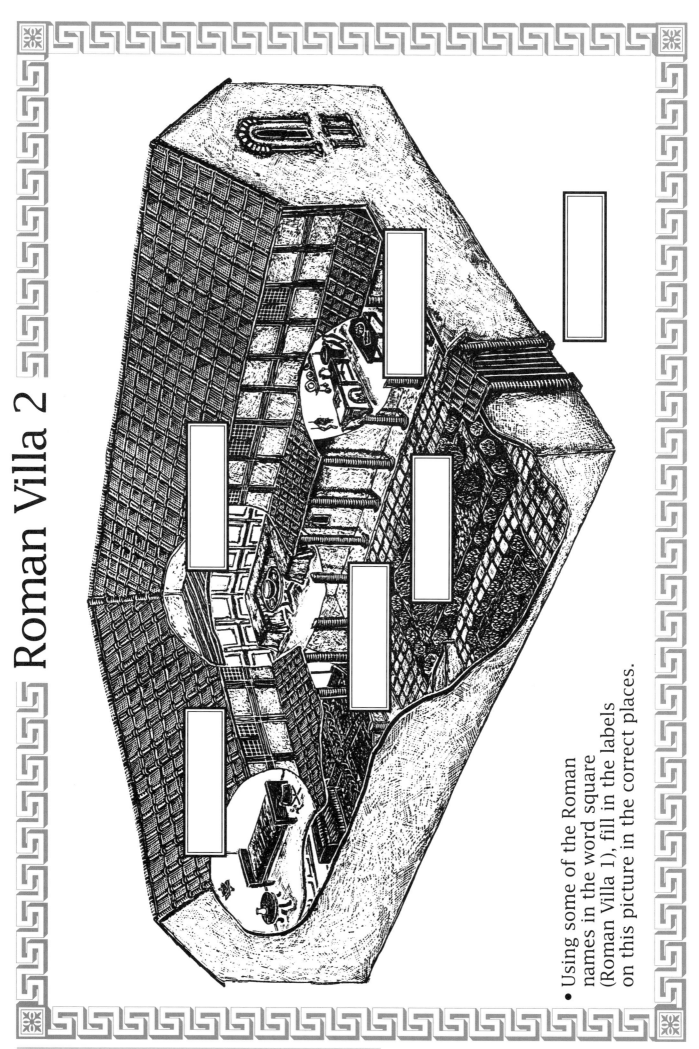

- Using some of the Roman names in the word square (Roman Villa 1), fill in the labels on this picture in the correct places.

Wax Writing Tablet

The Romans used a stylus (iron, pointed pen) to write on a wax tablet. Try making a writing tablet as shown here.

You will need the following equipment:
Wax (beeswax from a craft shop); balsa wood for the frame; wood block for base; iron stylus (Try a large nail. Will wood work?)

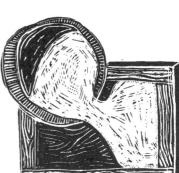

- Write your name on it.
- Write some Roman numbers.
- Which is easier to do? Why?
- What problems do you have to overcome?
- What might the Romans have done?

Mosaics

If you can spot any of the patterns, shown on this page, within the Roman floor in the photograph, join them up by drawing a line from one to the other.

Ivy leaf

Lotus flower

Wave, crested

Cantharus (urn)

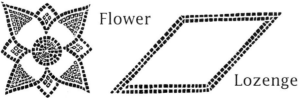
Flower

Lozenge

Guilloche chain

Greek key

- Using coloured paper make a tile design of your own.

You must use some of the Roman patterns.

Toga

These statues show us what kind of clothes the Romans wore. Study the pictures and describe them in your own words.

The main garment was called a toga. Here is how you put one on.

- Use an old curtain or sheet and try to put a toga on a friend.
- Can you think of some good points (advantages) as well as some bad things (disadvantages) about wearing a toga?

Shops

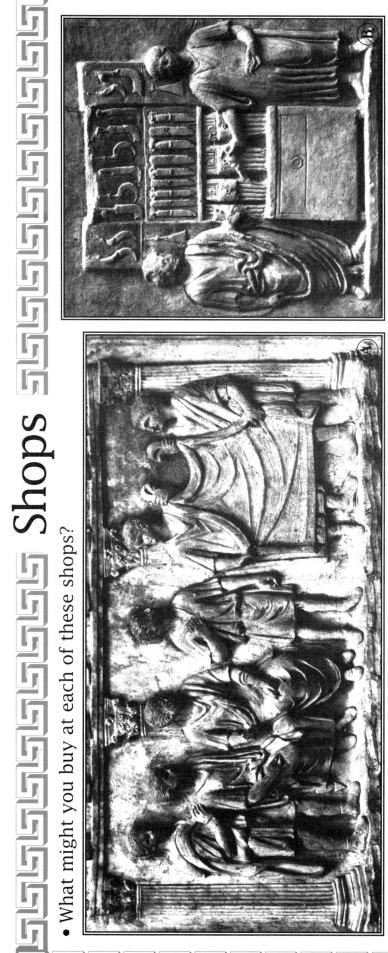

- What might you buy at each of these shops?

- Draw or make an arcade of Roman shops showing the shop fronts and the goods for sale. Most Roman shops had counters, which jutted out into the street.

A Taste of Rome

- From these foods, what would you use to sweeten something?
- Which food would you put into a salad?
- For what was the pestle and mortar used?

pestle and mortar

figs

grape juice

olives

dried peas

honey

dates

asafoetida

pine nuts

liquamen

mint

sage

basil

With your teacher's help, you could set up a tasting table so that you and your classmates could try some of these things.

Roman Kitchen

- Match these labels to the correct object.
  Say for what they were used.

SAMIAN WARE

AMPHORA

PESTLE AND MORTAR

SPOONS

STONE OVEN

KNIVES

Helping the Sick

- Explain how these surgical instruments might have been used.
- Try to find out what the Romans used to stop the pain during an operation.

Some of the medical words we use today came from Latin words used by the Romans. See if you can find English words, connected with health, which have come from these Latin ones:

ambulare   amputare

casus   doctus

hospitium   invalidus

medicus   opera

patiens

Spot the Gods

The Romans worshipped many gods. Each god stood for something different. Here is a list of some of them.

Study the pictures. Can you work out who is who?

BACCHUS (A)
The god of wine and drinking was

DIANA (D)
was the god of hunting

JUPITER (B)
was the chief god and controlled the elements, wind and weather

VENUS (E)
The goddess of love was

MERCURY (F)
was the messenger of the gods and was also the god of trading and thieving

JANUS (C)
could look at the past and at the future, he was the god of beginnings

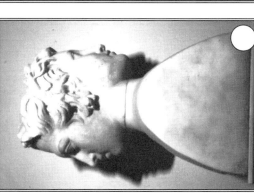
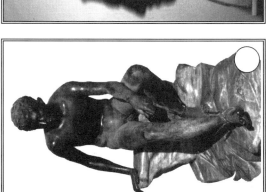
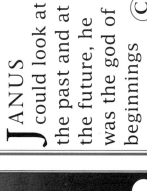
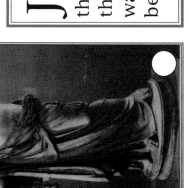
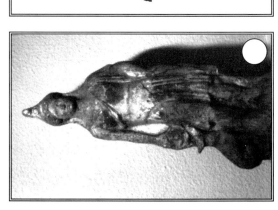

How did they do that?

Here are two examples of Roman technology.

- For what were they used? *Clue:* Look carefully at the circled pictures for the answers.
- Explain how they worked.

Country Life

List everything that is happening in this Roman picture.

Mystery Roman Objects Quiz

- Can you work out what these objects are?

1 These are as good as gold.

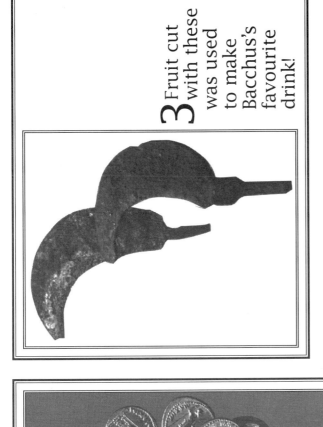

2 Put something in this and it might see you to bed.

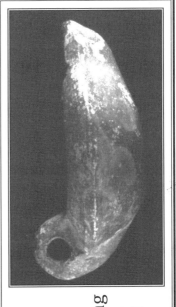

3 Fruit cut with these was used to make Bacchus's favourite drink!

4 A Roman word processor?

Roman Time Line

The Romans first came to Britain before Christ was born (BC).
Match these pictures and events.
Sort them into the right order. It will help if you cut them out.
Some things happened after Christ was born (AD), so be careful!

55BC —

The Roman legions left Britain to go to protect Rome.

54BC —

The building of Hadrian's Wall began. It was built to keep out the Picts.

AD43 —

Caesar returned with a bigger army then went back to Rome with prisoners.

Julius Caesar landed in Britain for the first time.

AD122 —

The Emperor Claudius invaded Britain. The Roman occupation of Britain began.

AD412 —

The Anglo-Saxons

In modern times the world is dominated by a Western culture, which owes a considerable debt to the Anglo-Saxons; yet the beginnings of the Anglo-Saxon world lie in the darkest part of the Dark Ages. The Anglo-Saxon 'period' has no clear beginning, like the Roman, and no clear end. It is a period of confusion in most adults' minds, consisting as it does, of many peoples and kingdoms, many kings, few dates and very little written evidence.

At the time of the recall of the legions, the population of these islands was very mixed. It included a large number of east Germans settled here by the Emperor Probus, and many other German auxiliary units positioned to defend the Empire. East Saxon cemeteries have been excavated near major Roman fortresses across the country testifying to their presence. By the middle of the fifth century the population of these islands included a large proportion of people of Germanic blood and speech.

After the retreat of the Romans, Saxon mercenaries continued to be employed by British rulers to keep the Picts and Scots at bay. But when they fell out with their employers, these mercenaries began the process of establishing their own Saxon kingdoms. When precisely this happened is not known, but the plain of York and the East Riding of Yorkshire became the kingdom of Deira (perhaps the first Saxon kingdom) in the sixth century. Its first king dated with any certainty is Aelli (AD558).

Loyalty to one's leader was most important in Saxon society, so the country inevitably took on a tribal character. As the Saxon kingdoms arose they generally acknowledged the most powerful king as 'bretwalda' (Britain ruler), but within the kingdoms tribal units remained. The names of the leaders and tribes are preserved in numerous place names. The obscure kingdom of Elmet is remembered in 'Barwick-in-Elmet' near Leeds; the Hwicce people in 'Wychwood' (wood of the Hwicce people). Glastonbury (the island of Glast's people) perpetuates Glast's name, and places ending in -ing are linked to the kinsmen of individuals whose names are constantly on our tongues but long since forgotten, hence; Haefer, Hicel and Tota (Havering, Hickling and Tooting). At Hastings resided Haesta's people and Wocca's people lived at Wokingham.

Whether they were North Folk, East Saxons, Feppingas, Stoppingas or Mercians, they were all Saxons to the Celts. All the invaders and settlers were of Germanic stock but both Angles and Saxons were happy to call themselves either, although even King Alfred proudly traced his origins to a particular Germanic tribe.

The Celts, under their British warlords, did not suddenly vanish when the Saxons took control, neither was that control gained overnight. Understandably perhaps, the Anglo-Saxon Chronicle does not record Saxon defeats by the British, but in the middle of the sixth century, central southern England was still being contested. The West Saxons fought against British armies at Old Sarum and Barbury Castle in Wiltshire during this period, and went on to contest territory with King Ethelbert of Kent. In AD577, three British kings were killed in a great battle against the Saxons at Dyrham above Bath and King Centwine eventually drove the British beyond Devon. But the British certainly did not all flee. A Welshman's value (*wergild*) is extensively recorded in Saxon annals and his presence confirmed in place names containing 'Lis' (chief's hall) and 'Walton' (Welshman's village).

After St Augustine (AD597), the Saxon conversion to Christianity began, and that it was to be of the Roman, not the Celtic sort, was secured by the Synod of Whitby (AD664). Saxon England contracted into fewer more powerful kingdoms. When Offa was king of Mercia as well as 'bretwalda', he ruled, from his capital in Tamworth, the tribes and kingdoms from the Thames to the Tyne and had the power and organisation to build the astonishing Dyke, 25 feet deep, 60 feet across, running from the Irish sea to the Bristol Channel. The boundaries of these ancient kingdoms still survive in some diocesan boundaries established during this period, which seem, perversely, not always to follow county lines.

Over many centuries, the Saxons fought the Welsh and each other for supremacy in Britain – then came the Vikings.

Notes on the photocopiables

Saxon Invaders (page 52)

A whole range of Germanic invaders attacked Britain from the east, Saxon, Jutish, Frankish and Frisian adventurers, who established themselves on the Saxon Shore. The names Essex, Middlesex, Sussex and Wessex are reminders of the East, Middle, South and West Saxons respectively. Numerous kingdoms were established. In the Midlands, the East, Middle and West Angles carved up the country between them. The Mercians, Deirans and Bernicians were all Angles, but the Celts generally called them all Saxons, as they were all of Germanic stock.

The children do not need to get lost in the complex detail about the kingdoms but the geographical origins of the invaders should be made clear.

- Project a copy of this map (make a transparency using a photocopier and then use an overhead projector) on to a board and trace a large wall map. Plot the invaders' routes and add explanatory labels.

- Examine a good modern map of Europe (most primary atlases will be too superficial; a good secondary or adult atlas would be best) and look for evidence of the invaders in place-names (not only Essex and Sussex but also Jutland and Saxony).

Anglo-Saxon Chronicle

(page 53)

A series of annals makes up the Chronicle. They plot the history of Britain, through Saxon eyes, from the period of Saxon migration to the reign of Stephen and are the most important documents on the period. English, not Latin, was the language chosen by the scribes who wrote it. Latin speakers had all but disappeared by the ninth century. The Chronicle is very concerned about chronology and the annals use the birth of Christ as the starting point for dating. 'A masterly innovation', as some historians have called it. Originally called 'Years of Grace', we now know them as 'Year of Our Lord, AD – *anno Domini*. At the time of the

Chronicle other methods of dating were still in use.

- Interrogate the quotations as evidence. Discuss authenticity and reliability.

- Make a Chronicle of Britain for one school year. (There will be opportunities to discuss the selection of news material, bias, honesty and error. Relate the work to the Saxon Chronicle.)

- Transcribe the extracts and illustrate them as a page from the Chronicle.

Evidence of the Saxons

(page 54)

By deduction, close observation and a process of elimination, children should arrive at the correct match. The full details are:

a A silver brooch. The cross is a clue to the owner's conversion to Christianity.

b This is a carefully reassembled mask helmet from the Sutton Hoo find currently in the British Museum. Note the eyebrows and the moustache. All the decorative panelling was worked in bronze. Early Saxon.

c The tower was built by the Saxons. A stone building was a rarity and the masons who built this may well have been brought over from Gaul.

d A comb and its case made from bone and antler horn.

- Make your own quiz sheet, using drawings or photographs of Saxon objects. Make up reasonable clues.

- Compile museum catalogue cards for each of the objects giving as much detail about each one as you can. In order to do quality work here children will need guidance. After discussion you might produce a proforma for the children to use giving the headings required; name, what it is made from, measurements, date, function, owner and so on.

- Draw up a production plan for someone to use to make one of these objects (say a bone comb). Explain stage by stage what has to be done. (Problem solving.)

Learning to be a Monk

(page 55)

The correct order is:

6, 3, 7, 8, 1, 4, 2, 5

- Enact as a class, a day in the life of a monk. Sometimes churches are willing to be come involved in a project like this. See *General Teaching Ideas*. The authors have been involved in 'Monk's Days' at Bristol and Salisbury cathedral and at Malmesbury Abbey, which were successful co-operative efforts. Contact your Diocesan Education Officer for help.

Sutton Hoo Treasure

(page 56)

Sutton Hoo was the tomb of a Saxon King. His coffin and treasures were placed in a special hut erected in the centre of his ship. Presumably the ship had been dragged from the River Deben near Woodbridge in Suffolk, to the 100 foot high ridge where the burial took place. The treasures, all of which are in the British Museum, are unsurpassed in quality and quantity, by any other Saxon find. The tomb dates from the seventh century and was discovered in 1939.

The length of this great gold buckle is 13.2cm and it weighs 414.6g. Animals, snakes and birds' heads, picked out in niello (a black compound of sulphur and silver, lead or copper) interweave in this complex design.

- Get the children to draw the outline of the buckle to its true size. Make a weight to equal that of the buckle.

- To what was this buckle attached? Draw an extension to the buckle as you imagine it would have been. Why has the rest of the object not survived?

Saxon Place-names (page 57)

The activity is self explanatory.

- How you use this will depend on your area. You might consider using a large county map and then place coloured map pins on Saxon settlements.

Alternatively use a map of England.

- To understand more clearly how the system worked, children could have fun making up place names using their own names. Follow the rules! For example, the settlement of Wocca's People is Wokingham.

Saxon Quiz (page 58)

Answer to the word search:

ALFRED: King Alfred the only king called 'Great'. Ruled Wessex; famously defeated the Vikings.

WERGILD: *Wergild* (or Wergeld) was literally a blood price, the price paid for killing that person. A good guide to social standing.

CHRONICLE: As in the Anglo-Saxon Chronicle, a kind of history linked to chronology.

WESSEX: The land of the West Saxons, varied according to waxing and waning power but centred on central southern England, Hampshire, Wiltshire and Dorset.

JUTES, SAXONS AND PICTS: Broadly, invaders from Jutland, Germany and Scotland

BEOWULF: One of the earliest and the longest complete Saxon poems to survive. It dates from the eighth century, when Saxon society was Christian and, clearly, relatively cultured. It is about the life and death of the monster Grendel.

The answers to the riddles are SHIELD and ICE.

- The children could make riddles of their own. They should conform to the Saxon style and relate to Saxon life. Compile a Riddle Book and decorate it with illuminated designs.

- Creating a *wergild* value list has possibilities. Be sensitive. What price a teacher?

Illuminated Manuscript

(page 59)

In the middle of the tenth century, 250 years after the Lindisfarne Gospels were written, a monk called, Aldred, wrote an Anglo-Saxon translation of the text alongside the original Latin. He also gave the provenance of the Gospels and a description:

'Eadfrith, Bishop of the Lindisfarne Church, originally wrote this book for God and Saint Cuthbert. And Ethelwald, Bishop of the Lindisfarne islanders, impressed it on the outside and covered it – as he well knew how to do. And Billfrith the anchorite, forged the ornaments that are on the outside and adorned it with gold and with gems and also with gilded over silver – pure metal. And Aldred, unworthy and most miserable priest, glossed it in English, between the lines, with the help of God and Saint Cuthbert.'

- Children can make illuminated initial letters for their own Saxon Riddles or, for example, a retelling of the Christmas Story. (Make sure that the children see some good colour examples first. Quality work is required. See *Resources* for suggested books.)

- A modern day 'illuminator' might be available to talk to the children and show them his/her craft. Illuminators are employed to produce special scrolls and to undertake signwriting projects or restoration work.

Anglo-Saxon Woman and Anglo-Saxon Man

(pages 60-61)

- If dressing-up is an option, try to replicate the dress using authentic materials (no polyester!). See the *History in Evidence* catalogue – address in *Resources*.

- A visit from an Anglo-Saxon group (see *Resources*) might be possible. If not, show slides available from West Stow.

- Make a Saxon Village frieze, getting the whole class to contribute people to fix on the village backdrop. Mount the figures proud of the background for greater effect.

- Build up a collage picture of a man or woman. Choose the correct materials and colours. You could enlarge this photocopiable sheet to give a large figure on which children can stick their materials.

Anglo-Saxon Gods (page 62)

In France the days of the week still have names traceable to Roman gods, hence *mardi* (Tuesday); *mercredi* (Wednesday); *jeudi* (Thursday); and *vendredi* (Friday). In Britain the Anglo-Saxon gods dominate, hence *Tiw* (Tuesday); *Woden* (Wednesday); *Thunor* (Thursday); and *Frig* (Friday).

Christian festivals clearly coincide with festivals of more ancient or heathen origin. Little is known of the Saxon god Eostre but the name lives on in the name of Easter.

- Compose stories or poems about the gods to illustrate their characters.

- Investigate words with origin in the gods or God. For example, 'Goodbye'.

- Make a Saxon calendar of one week. Illustrate each day with the acts of the gods.

Saxon Gameboard (page 63)

This activity is usually greatly enjoyed, especially by older juniors. It is best done in pairs and it requires time. The real test is when a child tries to play another child's game.

Battle of Maldon (page 64)

Just below Maldon on the Blackwater estuary in Essex, there is a causeway passable at low tide. Here, or hereabouts, the Battle of Maldon was fought in August 991. Byrhtnoth led the Anglo-Saxons (English) and Justin and Guthmund led the Vikings. The Vikings managed to cross the causeway and kill Byrhtnoth. Apart from a group of warriors, who fought to the death around Byrhtnoth's body, the English withdrew. The poem may have been written to encourage resistance to the Vikings as an alternative to the payment of Danegeld (protection money), which was common at that time. The spacing in the Anglo-Saxon/Old English version reflects the fact that it was put together from fragments.

- Teach the children about alliteration (front rhymes) and write alliterative verse. Why use alliteration?

- Mime the action of the battle (it need not be done in costume). Choose suitable music, or compose music, to accompany it (build on untuned percussion).

King Alfred's Jewel (page 65)

The smaller jewel (2.3cm diameter) was found at Minster Lovell near Oxford and may well have been made by the same craftsman who made the Alfred jewel (6.2 by 3.1 by 1.3cm) found a few miles from Athelney in the Somerset levels. The hole in the base of each suggests that a rod was inserted there and that these were therefore *aestels*, or book markers, for use when reading a manuscript. King Alfred almost certainly commissioned his jewel which is largely made of gold. Enclosed by the gold backplate is a rock crystal covering the figure worked in blue and green cloisonné enamel (the enamel fills in between an outline of flattened wire). It can be seen, together with the Minster Lovell jewel, in the Ashmolean Museum, Oxford.

- If they are not pointers (we are not certain), what are they? Ask the children to come up with plausible answers.

- Tell the story of how the Alfred Jewel became lost in the Althelney marshes (close to where Alfred hid from the Danes).

- Challenge the children to devise a way of making a copy of these *aestels* for use in the classroom.

A Saxon Winter (page 66)

This picture comes from a manuscript (ms Cotton Claudius BIV f29v) held in the British Library, London. The animals were killed because of the lack of feed for the winter, but nothing would have been wasted.

- Use speech balloons, or another form of annotation, to explain what is happening in the picture.

- Get a group of children to act out this scene. It could be scripted or unscripted. What happens next?

- What happens to livestock on British farms during the winter today? Make then and now friezes.

Beowulf and the Monster Grendel (page 67)

Here is a fine opportunity for imaginative work. Through the written word, drama, art, music and dance, the story of Beowulf can be dramatically presented. Use one of the fine retellings, available for children (see *Resources*) to capture the children's imagination. The story can be made into a complete class play with different acts and scenes. It can be told in a zig-zag cartoon (involves the children in sequencing the events as well). The monster can be built three dimensionally, painted, suspended, before being hanged, drawn and quartered!

Saxon Invaders

In the north Picts and Scots attacked what was left of Roman Britain. Angles, Saxons and Jutes attacked from the east. The Celts gradually escaped to the west and Wales. New Anglo-Saxon kingdoms came into being.

- From where did the invaders come?
- What do we call these places today? (Use an atlas.)
- Can you explain how the names Sussex, Essex and East Anglia came about?

Anglo-Saxon Chronicle

In the year of Christ's Nativity 494, Cerdic and Cynric landed with five ships. These were the first kings who conquered the land of Wessex from the Welsh.

The island of Britain is 800 miles long and 200 miles broad. There are five languages: English; British or Welsh; Irish, Pictish and Latin.

Hengest and Horsa (Saxons), invited Vortigern, king of the Britons, came to Britain at a place which is called Ebbsfleet (in Kent) at first to help the Britons, but later they fought against them.

- Write down all the facts that the Anglo-Saxon Chronicle tells us about Britain and the Saxon invaders. Find Ebbsfleet on a map.
- Put them in order. Start with those facts you think are most likely to be true; end up with those about which you are doubtful.
- Why should we have doubts about the truth of the Chronicle?

Evidence of the Saxons

Here are some of the things that the Saxons left behind.

- Match the pictures to the correct description.

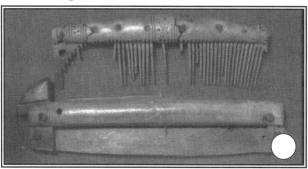

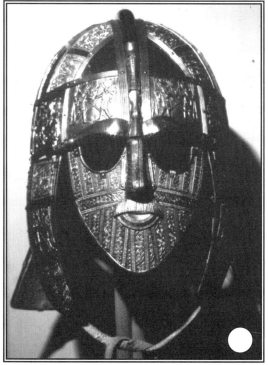

a This was found in the grave of a Saxon lady. You can tell that she was a Christian.

b This was made of bronze and worn for protection by somebody important.

c The tower was built by the Saxons, but the time was added later!

d Made from antler and bone. The teeth do not bite.

Learning to be a Monk

This is the story of a Saxon boy who became a monk. The pictures are not in the right order.

• Cut them out and arrange them correctly.　• Colour them and stick them in your book.

4 After *Prime* came breakfast then lessons until *Terce* at 9.00 am. He wrote his letters on a wax tablet.

3 His bed was in a dormitory with other boys. At 6.00 am he was awake and at church for *Prime*.

2 He went to church seven times a day. *Nocturns* was the first service at 2.00 am.

1 A boy was taken to the monastery by his parents. He usually stayed there forever.

8 He went to three more services; *Nones* 3.00 pm; *Vespers* 6.00 pm and *Compline* at 7.00 pm. Then he went to bed.

7 In the afternoon there were more lessons. Singing, writing, reading and praying.

6 After *Sext* at midday he ate a meal in silence. It was vegetarian food.

5 He wore a rough woollen robe. He worked in the fields, milked the cows or went fishing in the morning.

Sutton Hoo Treasure

About sixty years ago an Anglo-Saxon ship
was found buried with lots
of treasure at Sutton Hoo
in Suffolk. It was the
grave of a king of
the East Angles,
probably
King
Raewald.

This great gold
buckle was one
of the finds.

- Can you
  follow the
  twisting snakes?
- Use gold (yellow)
  and black to colour
  the buckle. Mount
  it on to black paper.

Saxon Place-names

- Use a map of Britain to find places which contain these Saxon words.
- In which part of the country do you think would be best to look?

Saxon word	Meaning	Places
borough or burgh	fortified settlement	Marlborough, Edinburgh
dene, den	valley	_____
ey, ea	river	_____
field, feld	field	_____
ford	river crossing	_____
ham	settlement	_____
holt	wood	_____
ing	people	_____
leigh, lea or ley	clearing in the woods	_____
mere	lake	_____
sted	place	_____
stow or stoke	meeting place	_____
ton or tun	farm	_____
wick, wic or wich	farm settlement	_____
worth	land fenced or hedged	_____

Scroll Search (word square).

- Find the words listed. They are buried in the square on the scroll.

R	E	C	E	A	C	I	B	E
F	L	U	W	O	E	B	E	L
R	A	X	E	S	S	E	W	C
A	L	F	R	E	D	A	H	I
U	J	U	G	A	E	L	E	N
P	U	P	I	C	T	S	A	O
N	T	A	L	R	A	H	U	R
L	E	A	D	E	G	I	L	H
O	S	A	X	O	N	A	A	C

JUTES

SAXON

PICTS

WESSEX

ALFRED

WERGILD

CHRONICLE

BEOWULF

- Who or what were they?

Saxon Riddles

What am I?

- ❧ I am one on my own.

- ❧ I am wounded by weapon of iron, scarred by sword, exhausted from the edges of the blade.

- ❧ I often see battle and fight the foe.

- ❧ I have never found a doctor that could heal my wounds with herbs.

A wondrous thing happened at sea. The water turned to bone.

Say what it was.

Illuminated Manuscript

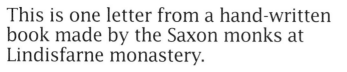

This is one letter from a hand-written book made by the Saxon monks at Lindisfarne monastery.

- Can you find any creatures? Try to draw one of the patterns carefully. Colour it using only orange, red, green, blue and black. Time how long it takes you to do it well.

- How long do you think it might have taken for the monk to draw it?

Anglo-Saxon Woman

Make clear labels for this drawing to explain what she is wearing.

Colour the picture. Read the description first!

Women wore clothing in layers, one on top of the other. Under-clothes were linen, top garments usually wool. Colours were mostly blue, blue/grey, brown, green, yellow and off-white. Dresses were made from rectangles of cloth fastened by brooches at the shoulders. Beads and jewellery were sometimes worn. A belt helped to stop the clothes dragging on the ground. Children were dressed like little adults.

Anglo-Saxon Man

Make clear labels to explain
how this Saxon man was dressed.
Colour the picture correctly.
Read the description
before you start.

A man's shirt was called a cyrtel. As fashions changed the cyrtel got longer. Breeches or leggings were also worn and they had socks sewn to them. A rich man might wear a leather waistcoat over his cyrtel and have a helmet and sword. Carrying a spear showed that you were a free man. Cloaks were worn in bad weather. Green, brown, blue, grey, yellow and off-white were the main colours used for clothes.

Anglo-Saxon Gods

The Romans named the days of the week after their gods.
One European language still uses these names.
Which one?

mardi 1	mercredi 2	jeudi 3	vendredi 4
the day of Mars	the day of Mercury	the day of Jove	the day of Venus

_ _ _ _ day   _ _ _ _ _ _ day   _ _ _ _ _ day   _ _ _ day

The Anglo-Saxons did the same.
We still use some of the names.

• Work out which days are named after:

Tiw 1	Woden 2	Thunor 3	Frig 4
a god of battle	the chief war god	god of thunder	goddess of fertility

_ _ _ _ day   _ _ _ _ _ _ day   _ _ _ _ _ day   _ _ _ day

• Write in the missing letters
  to make up the correct words.

An important Christian festival takes its name
from the Saxon god Eostre.
• Which festival?

There are 50 places named after Saxon gods,
like Thundersley (Thunor) and Wednesbury (Woden).
• Write down any more places you find.

Saxon Gameboard

- Complete this board to make a game of your own.
- Add events that might have happened to any Saxon family (falling ill, having a feast or killing a wolf).

Start

Saxon warriors fight the Picts and Scots 449 (have another go)

The monk Bede dies 735 (lose three places)

Viking Great Army raids England 865 (go back to the beginning)

Saxons defeat the British at Dyrham 577 (gain one square)

St Augustine landed in Kent 597 (move forward two squares)

Viking kingdom makes Jorvik (York) its capital 876 (miss a go)

King Alfred defeats the Danes (Vikings) 878 (gain three places)

Finish

Battle of Maldon

In AD991 the Saxons fought the Vikings on a causeway in Essex.
The Saxon leader Byrhtnoth was killed and a group
of Saxon warriors fought to the death around his body.
This is part of a Saxon poem about the end of the battle.
Add a few lines of your own to finish the story.

'Hige sceal þe heardra, heorte þe cenre,
mod sceal þe mare, þe ure mægen lytlað.
Her lið ure ealdor eall forheawen,
god on greote; a mæg gnornian
se ðe nu fram þis wigplegan wendan þenceð.
Ic eom frod feores; fram ic ne wille,
ac ic me be healfe minum hlaforde,
be swa leofan men, licgan þence.'
Swa hi Æþelgares bearn ealle bylde,
Godric, to guþe; oft he gar forlet,
wælspere windan on þa wicingas;
swa he on þam folce fyrmest eode,
heow and hynde, oð þæt he on hilde gecranc.

'The will shall be harder, the courage shall be keener
    Spirit shall grow great, as our strength falls away.
Here our lord lies, mangled and struck dead.
    A good man prostrate: all his life shall he lament
That warrior who flies from this battle-death and glory.
    Aged am I, yet I will not turn at the end
But was born to lie dead by my patron,
    So dear a master — '

Also the son of Ethelgar summoned them all,
    Godric was his name, to new feats of fierceness
Often he sent a spear veering into the Vikings.
    Even he went first, feinting and fighting
Till he lay spent of life on the lost field.

King Alfred's Jewel

The Alfred Jewel was found in the Somerset marshes close to where King Alfred once hid from the Vikings. It is gold with a green and blue enamelled figure.

On it is written

AELFRED MEC HEHT
GEWYRCAN
which means
'Alfred had me made'.

Both of these jewels were probably pointers used when reading from a book so something must be missing.

- What do you think it is?
- Can you complete the pointers and add colour to the jewels?

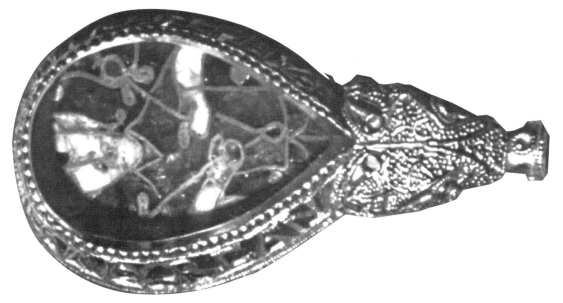

A Saxon Winter

There was not enough food to feed all the animals through winter.

Look at the picture evidence.

- What happened to many of the animals?
- How did they use them?
- Explain what happened next. You could draw your own pictures.

Beowulf and the Monster Grendel

Beowulf is a Saxon story poem about the fight between a man-eating monster called Grendel, and a Saxon warrior hero, Beowulf, who had the strength of ten men.

One night, Grendel came out of the marshes and burst into the hall where Beowulf and his men were sleeping. The foul-smelling monster was ten feet tall with skin like a lizard. It padded into the room. The men drew their swords, but Grendel seized the first man and tore him in two. It seemed that no sword could pierce Grendel's thick skin. Then Beowulf wrestled him. Suddenly there was a scream of agony, and the monster fled to the marshes to die. Nothing was left but a trail of blood and the monster's arm held firmly in Beowulf's iron grasp.

• Add the monster to this picture.

Vikings

In spite of recent adjustments to our views on the Vikings, (emphasis is increasingly placed on the fact that they belonged to a vigorous mercantile community which was remarkably democratic; that they had considerable skill as craftsmen and ship builders and that they travelled widely even as far as North America), it is hard to escape the view that they were cruel, barbaric heathens. The best sources from the period promote this view but then they are Anglo-Saxon and Christian so we must expect some bias.

Nevertheless, evidence from all over Europe confirms that, in spite of the extensive cultural achievements of the Vikings, they were indeed a vigorous, barbaric race. They were not just small-time raiders; large Viking armies defeated the national armies of many European kingdoms. They terrified the inhabitants of these islands and almost wiped out learning in England. The logic of their culture – which extolled warrior virtues and brave death – justified their particularly cruel treatment of prisoners, regardless of sex or age. A number of defeated Saxon kings, captured in battle, had their lungs spread out before them while still alive. A brave enemy needs every opportunity to show his courage; so it was argued.

The Viking imprint was placed on Britain over a period of some 300 years, beginning with the first raids for plunder made during the early 790s. As the Normans who conquered England in 1066 were themselves 'northmen' who had settled in France, one could argue that Viking influence extended over an even longer period.

Within 90 years of the first raids, the Vikings had subjugated the three great kingdoms of Mercia, Northumbria and East Anglia and had turned their attention on the only one remaining, Wessex. In 870 a large Danish army, from its base in Reading, set out across the Berkshire Downs. At Ashdown, not far from the Uffington horse, (east of the modern town of Swindon), King Aethelred, and his young brother Alfred, defeated the Danes with great slaughter.

But the Vikings were to return to make a surprise attack on Chippenham in the New Year 878. Alfred, now king, with no standing winter army, was forced to hide in the Somerset levels and to rely for a while, on hit and run tactics. How Alfred was able to co-ordinate the forces available in the west from Dorset, Devon and Hampshire, we do not know, but in the early summer he did battle with the Danish king, Guthrum, at Edington near Warminster in Wiltshire. The Saxon victory was a famous one and the Danes were forced back to the north and east of England, although the permanency of 'Danelaw' was now recognised by Alfred.

Battles with the Danes continued after Alfred's death, as did struggles for the throne of Wessex. More Viking settlers, this time mainly Norwegian, crossed from Ireland to settle in the North West, particularly the Wirral peninsula. Alfred's system of building boroughs, or fortified towns, as a defence against raiders, was revised and extended. Edward the Elder, Alfred's son, gained supremacy over all of England, south of the Humber.

The last independent Scandinavian power in England ended with the defeat and death of Eric Bloodaxe (AD954), whose kingdom had been based on York (Jorvik). In the early part of the eleventh century, leading English and Danish leaders were able to agree to live together in peace, although the real threat of Scandinavian invasion and domination remained up to and including the year of the Norman Conquest.

The Viking legacy is considerable. The Vikings affected the pattern of settlement in England, the nature of government, our traditions and language. The very common place-names that end in -by and -thorpe are Scandinavian, and if you refer to your husband, or use the words, die, ill, skill or skin, you are bearing witness to the Viking legacy.

Notes on the photocopiables

Viking Voyages (page 75)

Viking culture saw great virtue in fighting, so one of the reasons why the Vikings attacked not only Britain, but countries across the known world, was the quest for adventure, glory and booty. They were great explorers and shrewd traders. Population growth and the pressure on land, which also contributed to Viking dispersal, are not fully understood.

They attacked Britain and Ireland from every direction, harried France and Spain, sailed into the Mediterranean, sought land and booty in Asia Minor, and even ventured into modern Iraq, via Russian rivers and the Black Sea. A Viking settlement has been positively confirmed at L'Anse aux Meadows in Newfoundland, so the first European foot on North American soil was almost certainly a Viking one and it made its imprint around the year AD1000. Newfoundland may well have been the Vinland (land where grapes grew), referred to in Viking sagas.

- Extend the worksheet activity by looking at the routes and directions and calculate distances. What would have been the main problems faced en route? (Bear in mind the type of vessels used.)

- Plan a Viking raid on Britain. What would you need to take with you? How would you travel?

- Tell the story of a Viking journey as if you were one of the crew.

Viking Place-names (page 76)

A pattern should emerge, that roughly corresponds with settlement concentrated within the extent of Danelaw. The area into which the resistance of Wessex confined the Viking invaders, ran north of a line that approximates to the modern A5 trunk road from London to Holyhead. Scandinavian words still linger, particularly in the language of North-East England, and survive in some of the more obscure Yorkshire dialect words.

- Study a Viking settlement, for example, Jorvik.

- Build a model of a settlement based upon Jorvik. Give it an appropriate Viking name.

The Vikings are coming!
(page 77)

The Vikings seemed to have thoroughly terrorised the Saxons. As heathens they had no respect for churches, such as Lindisfarne. This made their crimes seem all the more heinous to the Christian Saxons. The Saxons talked about the 'fury of the northmen' and of 'murdering wolves'. The word Viking means pirate. The most common name for them all, whether from Sweden, Denmark or Norway, was simply northmen.

- Tell the story of the Lindisfarne raid. This could be written in the style of a report of an official Public Inquiry, or alternatively, as a front page tabloid newspaper story.

- Write the chronicle of a Lindisfarne monk, who managed to escape the slaughter.

- Paint or crayon a series of pictures to tell the story of the raid from start to finish.

Viking Saga: the Murder!
(page 78)

Sagas were probably first transmitted orally. The greatest of the Icelandic Sagas, *Njal's Saga*, dates from the end of the thirteenth century but relates to events that happened three hundred years earlier. The written tradition probably started in Iceland, early in the twelfth century. The saga, part of which is adapted for this sheet, is full of casual violence which builds to violent enmity and the burning alive of a revered farmer and wise man, Njal, in his home with his family.

- Have a class discussion about violence. What might have caused the Vikings to be such a violent people?

- Some children might like to make up a saga of their own in cartoon form. (Useful ordering and sequencing practice.) It could also be done, co-operatively, as an audio tape with sound effects.

Evidence Underground

(page 79)

Make sure that the sketches build on the evidence. You could try extending the drawing of the photograph itself. Get the children to think about eating and sleeping on board ship.

Viking ships moved by wind and muscle power, although the evidence in this picture does not prove this. Each ship carried a number of oar-spaces (or rooms) according to size and function. A crew of thirty men was about standard for most ships and they sat on chests filled with their belongings.

- You can stress the incomplete nature of archaeological evidence by a number of activities. Giving children part of a broken pot and getting them to reconstruct the original from it (by drawing) works well. (Make your own shards and keep a copy of the pot you used to show to the children after they have produced their own sketches based upon the shards.)

- Use a computer simulation such as 'Dig Out' (Available from AVP – see *Resources*) to give the children the feel of archaeological work.

- You may be able to visit a working dig. Contact local groups or English Heritage. The English Heritage magazine for teachers often has good ideas for archaeological projects.

Archaeological Finds

(page 80)

The objects are:

1 A *leather* tenth-century boot found in York.
2 An *iron* stirrup, with brass inlay, found in Battersea, London.
3 *Wooden* spindle with a *stone* whorl.
4 *Bone* strap-end with a stranded plait design

- Detailed sketches of the objects can be made.

- Try making copies of some of the objects for a Viking artefact display.

- Make up a story about how all these objects might have come together. Imagine that they were found on an archaeological dig.

- The exploits of a great archaeologist could be the focus of a drama day or a subject for creative writing.

Inside a Viking (page 81)

Children will no doubt appreciate that McDonald's hamburgers had not been invented in the first millennium. Also unknown to the Vikings were: potatoes, chocolate, tea and coffee. The reason for this is that the New World (the Americas) provided these foods and the New World had yet to be discovered and explored by Europeans.

Viking mealtimes were unlikely to have had clockwork regularity, but they seemed to have eaten twice a day, breakfast and dinner. They were big fish and meat eaters (mutton, beef, seal, horse and so on). Consumption in the winter included salted and pickled foods preserved from the autumn. Nuts, fruit, vegetables and milk products such as butter were eaten as well. Water and milk were drunk as well as mead; a strong alcoholic drink made from honey. Bread was also a staple part of their diet. Food was eaten from wooden bowls with fingers, spoons and knives. Forks had not been invented.

- Chart the staple foods of today. Let the whole class keep a tally of what they eat in a full week (concentrate on the basic foodstuff – what it is made from – not the brand name). Compare the list with a Viking one.

- Prepare a display of Viking food. Use pictures if this proves difficult to manage.

- Hold a Viking Market to the sounds of Viking music (see *Resources*) and get the children to barter for produce.

- Experiment with different methods of food preservation, for example, drying; salting; pickling. Use dried beans and wheat. Examine preserves and chutneys.

Picture Reading (page 82)

Part of Eric Bloodaxe's kingdom has been recreated *in situ* underground in York, the

Viking capital of Jorvik. It is of such a reconstruction that this picture was taken.

The children should fill in the blank labels on the picture as follows:

drinking – drinking horn in the man's hand.

cooking and/or **keeping warm** – fire where cooking is taking place.

storing – two places: containers in the centre foreground and storage sacks hanging up.

keeping warm – blanket round the man's shoulders.

- Make a chart showing 'What they did then' and 'What we do now' comparisons of domestic arrangements. (The lavatory – you may well be asked – was an outside latrine shielded by a wicker screen. Archaeologists have excavated them in York.)

- Pretend to be a Health and Safety Officer and write a report on a visit to a Viking house.

Vikings Top and Bottom

(pages 83-84)

Top dog was the king or ruler. Fighting prowess was the most valued quality and he was expected to lead by example and not be outdone in valour by any of his men. His position depended upon it. Other leaders had a similar role and were expected to share his warrior qualities. They were called Jarls. The middle echelon of society consisted of farmers (bondi), fishermen and traders. They were the backbone of society and it was these men who formally handed over the keys of the house to the women and went off to conquer, trade and seek booty during the period of Viking expansion.

Bottom of the heap were the thralls or servants. There were slaves too, captured during fighting expeditions, but there seems to have been little to choose between the life of a slave and that of a thrall.

There were a whole range of other members of society, who are largely invisible to us except through saga and fragmentary evidence. Women, as well as teachers, poets and craftsmen must have been essential to sustain the vitality of the Viking age. In legend, the wives of Jarls were beautiful and charming and

farmer's wives were active, capable people charged with all the responsibilities of managing the household.

- Make power diagrams of a social group with which the children are familiar. The school is a good starting point. Who has the power?

- Discuss why so little is heard of Viking women.

- Write pen portraits of each group in the diagram and make a large illustrated chart for display.

Viking Time Line (page 85)

What has been said about other time lines in this book (see pages 5, 13 and 46) also applies here. Children should have a visual *aide memoire* to help them place events in time. Precise dating is not important, order and sequence certainly are. Use pictures as much as possible and get the children to create their own time lines, which can be manipulated and added to.

Using Living Things (page 86)

As with all early societies, survival was the most pressing concern of the Vikings. They were skilled at making the maximum use of natural harvests for keeping warm and keeping fed. All the animals were hunted for food as a supplement to the meat provided by domestic livestock. (Soups and stews were standard Viking fare.) Moreover, when on the move, they did not keep domestic livestock. Animal skins were used for clothing. Leather was a particularly important commodity and furs were essential in the Viking homelands where winters were very hard. Bone, horn and antler were used to make tools, knife handles, combs and drinking cups. Even the membrane that covered a new born calf could be used as a primitive window pane to let light into Viking houses.

It is expected that the children will understand that the animals might be put to several uses. The sorting exercise lends itself to a Venn diagram presentation.

- How do we use these creatures today? Make a chart.

- Classify a child's clothing and equipment according to whether the items are made from natural or man-made materials. How many are of animal origin?

- How many Vikings would belong to animal rights organisations? Why not? Debate.

Viking Ships (page 87)

Viking ships were plank boats constructed by overlapping planking (clinker built) fastened together by clenched nails. The central keel plank was not a true keel because it was not deeper than it was wide. This made the boat particularly good for coastal waters. Moss and tarred wool were used to fill in the cracks between the planking. Cross beams tied the boat together. Steering was by way of a steer-board or oar lashed to the side stern of the ship. It had a central mast.

No Viking project would be complete without the building of a model longship. There are a variety of ways of doing this. It is best to decide first the purpose of building the ships. Are they for display? To tell a story? Illustrate a point? If they are built to help the children understand more about how these boats were built, then you must take care about scale, construction techniques and materials.

- Challenge the children to make a simple boat that not only floats but which can be propelled by wind power. (How can you provide a consistent wind?)

- Build models out of two halves of a polystyrene meat container (as supplied in supermarkets). Clearly a material such as balsa wood is preferable, but not so easy to use. OR

- Construct a wooden keel from wooden strips sawn by hacksaw and stuck together to get the correct shape. Stick overlapping planking – in the Viking style – on to the frame. Use thin balsa sheets or cardboard and a glue gun (safety precautions apply). OR

- Make a classroom-size reproduction, using sheets of card or corrugated roll, over a frame of old chairs and desks or large boxes. Equip the boat properly and use for drama and role play. OR

- Measure out the dimensions of a Viking ship on the playground and mark in thick chalk.

Viking Warriors and Weapons (page 88)

Viking society was a warrior society. All males were expected to maintain weapons, train and keep fit for war. The wealthy Jarls spent a great deal of the wealth on equipping themselves with excellent weapons. Shields were made of planks and swords were made of iron. Some beautifully decorated swords, with hilts embellished with brass and silver, have been discovered. Swords, spears and axes were the main offensive weapons. Berserkers were a particularly frenetic breed of warriors who flew into a kind of hypnotic rage and had no fear in battle. It seems likely that this was drug-induced (possibly fly agaric). Whatever caused them to go berserk, even other Vikings were wary of them.

- Make and display the kit of a Viking warrior.

- Make a frieze of a Viking raid making sure that all the warriors are properly dressed and equipped.

- Make a single item of equipment as accurately as you can, for example, helmet, sword, shield. Work from good picture references.

Runes (page 89)

Runes are Viking writing. They take the form that they do because the linear shapes of the letters can easily be carved on wood or stone. The shortest runic alphabet had 16 letters, although an earlier one had 24. It is this alphabet, that is called the *futhark* after the appearance of the first six letters. Rune stones can be found all over Scandinavia, and are a major source of information about the Vikings. Some of the rune stones are decorated with patterns in red, blue, black and white paint. They convey information, commemorate loved ones and mark boundaries. The Vikings left rune graffiti almost everywhere they went.

The skill of rune writing was highly admired and a man who knew the runes was believed to have acquired a magical power.

- Paint a rune stone. Make accurate patterns and use the correct colours.

- Try carving runes using small chisels on wood. (Safety precautions apply.)
- Make runic messages for each other to decipher.

Children at Work and Play

(page 90)

Vikings played a board game called 'hnefatafl', built around the defence of a 'king'. Chess too was played by the Vikings, certainly in the twelfth century in Iceland and probably before then, elsewhere. Much of what children did to occupy their time was a copy of adult pastimes. The idea of childhood as a different culture may be considered a modern invention. Skills like that of weaving and spinning had to be learned and the learning started early. Story-telling (and listening to stories) was much enjoyed by Vikings and it was not just a pastime for children but a favoured accompaniment to feasting and celebration. Practising with swords and wrestling were clearly important adult activities.

Children also played with dolls, played chasing games and games on the snow and ice in their homelands. Skating on bone skates, and a bat and ball game were also enjoyed.

- Hold a Viking playtime where every child is involved in some Viking activity.
- Compare what the Vikings enjoyed with what children enjoy today. Look at the famous Brueghel painting *Children's Games* (available as a large picture in the Collins *Cross-Curricular Big Book*, 0 00 314153 5).
- Challenge the children to make a toy from natural objects found in the field and forest.

Viking Wallhanging: A Warrior (page 91)

The similarity between the Viking warrior on horseback and mounted warriors shown on the Bayeaux tapestry is marked. Normans were originally Northmen or Norsemen so the craftsmen and culture behind both have the same origins. The tapestry shown on this photocopiable hangs in Baldishol Stave Church in Norway and it was made at the beginning of the twelfth century. Chain mail appears in this picture, so clearly the figure is from the very end of what might be called the Viking era.

- Provide labels for the warrior's clothes and equipment. They should explain what they are called and for what they are used.
- Display a copy of the Bayeaux tapestry for comparison. List as many points of similarity as you can find.
- Trace a similar design on to calico and stitch the outline in coloured cottons. Work as close to the original as possible. Check colours.

Gods (page 92)

Neither Vikings, Romans nor Saxons were originally monotheistic and this is something the children need to have explained to them. Viking beliefs bolstered and provided the rationale for the violence, which permeated that society. Their gods were not always on the side of right. It was as if teachers supported the playground bully instead of discouraging him. Viking gods could not be trusted, and might turn against their supporters with unexpected fury. Many of the myths associated with their gods were attempts by the Vikings to explain the harsh northern world from which they came, and which they did not really understand. The relationship of one myth to another does not form a tidy pattern of beliefs or theology, and many stories hardly connect with one another at all.

Viking Farm (page 93)

A Viking farm like this existed at Ribblehead in North Yorkshire. Excavations have enabled us to build a good picture of what the farm looked like and this artwork is based upon that. At Stong in Iceland, a full reconstruction of such a farm, complete with turf roof, has been made.

The main house is the largest. It was a long chamber with a narrow protected entrance and thick earth walls to keep out the weather. The second building, complete with roof hole (smoke does not readily exit through a hole in the roof but tends to blow back), in the kitchen. All three buildings were connected by a flagged path to ease access in all weathers. It is likely that the third building was some kind of workshop. The children should be able to make reasonable guesses as to the building materials used, except perhaps for the roof which was usually a turf one. Animals, such as goats, frequently sought to feed on these roofs which had very easy low access.

- Start with the wooden frame and build a good size reconstruction of a Viking farm. All the material should be authentic, although the joining of the wood is best done by using modern glue. (This will make a good challenge for design/technology. Pre-cut wood as supplied for school technology projects, should be used for the frame construction.)

- Imagine what it was like to live in one of these houses for a complete day and night. Pretend that you travel through time and have to do just that. Describe what it is like.

Mystery Objects (page 94)

The mystery objects are:

1 The hilt of a Viking sword. The swords were made of iron but the hilts of the more valuable prized examples were decorated with bronze and, as in this case, silver. It is about 1000 years old and has an English style curved sword guard. The entire blade of this example has survived and it is kept in the Prehistoric Museum, Moesgard.

2 A shallow iron pan. The base is sagging slightly, but it has been made from a single sheet of metal. The handle was formed by twisting two iron rods together and welding them at one end. Made in the late ninth century and discovered during the building of the Cathedral car park in Winchester.

3 A stirrup. Fourteen examples similar to this have been found in Britain mainly within the area that was once known as Danelaw.

4 Silver ring and pin brooch. This is Danish and was found in Jutland, but many of this type have been found in England and Scandinavia.

- Observing, drawing, researching and recording are suggested activities. (See similar object sheet suggestions for the Romans and the Saxons, pages 21 and 48).

- Interrogate the objects as evidence and wring as much information as possible out of them. What do they tell us about the people who made and used them?

- Give the children a number of authentic 'mystery' Viking smells to identify – a beeswax candle snuffed out; smoked fish and so on.

Bede's Book (page 95)

The Ecclesiastical History of the English People by the Venerable Bede, was copied many times in the Middle Ages and 160 copies survive. Four copies survive from the eighth century; the oldest are in Cambridge and Leningrad. These quotations are from a modern Penguin edition, although they were first printed in 1480. The lower picture is a nineteenth-century romanticised impression of a monk and scribe.

Bede was born in Wearmouth in AD673, and was brought up for a while in the monastery there. He moved to Jarrow at an early age and spent the rest of his life there. In AD716 the monasteries at Jarrow and Wearmouth contained 600 monks. They were solid stone-built establishments, decorated with panel paintings brought over from the continent. They were thriving centres of Christian culture. Bede's teaching, and his written works, relied heavily on the resources of the fine library. He wrote in Latin, a language he learned at Jarrow, and completed the history when he was about 60 years old. It is a church history, concerned mainly with the development of the English Church, but it also sheds light on political history and social comment. Bede died in AD735.

- Find out about life in a Saxon monastery. What did the monks actually do?

- Make a book about Saints. What is a saint? Decorate it with suitable designs. Examine contemporary designs for ideas.

Viking Voyages

Iraq

Turkey

Southern France

Spain

Greenland

Iceland

Britain and Ireland

North America (Vinland)

The Vikings were great travellers.

- Mark the routes you think that they probably took to reach these places? Remember they travelled by boat.

- Which was furthest from their homeland?

Viking Place-names

Villages and towns which end in:
- *by* (a farm or village)
- *thwaite* (a meadow or clearing)
- *thorpe* (a small settlement)
- *toft* (ground where houses were built)

were places where the Vikings settled.

Scunthorpe

Derby

- Look for these endings. Mark, with a cross on the map, as many places as you can find.
- Are there any near where you live?
- What do you notice?

The Vikings are coming!

The Saxons feared the Vikings. They wrote about them in a great Chronicle. The Chronicle says:

Year AD 793

A little after, in the same year, the heathen destroyed God's church in Lindisfarne with great slaughter.

I n this year terrible portents appeared over Northumbria and miserably frightened the inhabitants. Exceptional flashes of lightning and fiery dragons were seen flying in the air.

- Look up the meanings of the words: chronicle   portents   slaughter
- Did the Saxons really see flying dragons?
- Draw your own pictures to fit the words from the Chronicle.

Viking Saga: the Murder!

Sigmund and Skjold gathered together a group of armed men and rode off to ambush Thord. When Sigmund saw Thord coming, he shouted, 'Give up Thord, for now is your time to die!'

'Never! I will kill you in single combat,' said Thord.

'We are not fools,' answered Sigmund, 'We shall use our advantage in numbers to overcome "Sharp-killer" your sword.'

Thord defended himself well and Sharp-killer shattered both their spears.

Then Skjold hacked off Thord's arm.

Thord bravely fought on with the other arm for some time.

Finally Sigmund ran him through with his sword and Thord fell dead on the ground.

Sigmund and Skjold covered his body with turf and stones.

• Make up some more of this saga.
  Add your own drawings to illustrate it.

Evidence Underground

This belonged to the Vikings. It was found buried beneath a mound of earth.

- Can you work out what it must have looked like when it was first made? Draw sketches.

- How did it move?
- How can you tell?
- Why do you think it was buried?

Archaeological Finds

Archaeologists found these in the ground.
Stone, leather, bone, iron and wood were used to make them.

• Use your best guesses to complete this chart.

Object	What is it?	From what is it made?	What does it tell us about the people who used it?

Inside a Viking

- Put these foods in the right stomachs. (Draw connecting lines.)

Some of them were not known to the Vikings.

- Can you find out why?

horsemeat

blackberries

mead

salted fish

tea

potatoes

coffee

peas

hamburger

plums

chocolate

nuts

onions

Picture Reading

Jorvik was the Viking town of York. This picture shows part of a Viking house which has been built inside the Jorvik Museum.

- Write the correct words into the blank labels.
- Describe how the Vikings kept warm, cooked and drank.

drinking

cooking

storing

keeping warm

Vikings Top and Bottom 1

Vikings were neither all equal nor all free.

- Cut out these people and put them into order of importance.
- Who was top Viking? Give reasons for your choices.

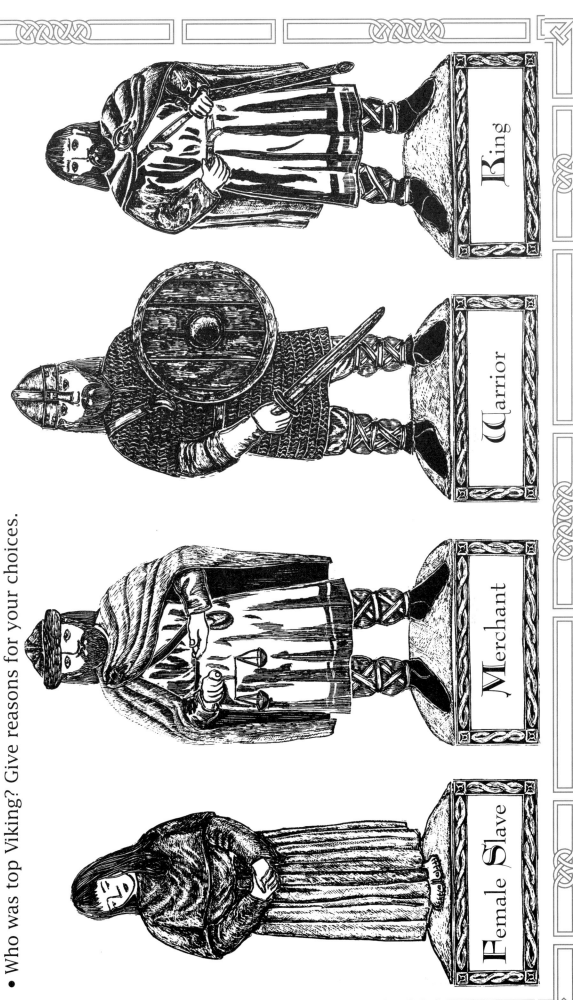

King

Warrior

Merchant

Female Slave

Vikings Top and Bottom 2

Vikings were neither all equal nor all free.
- Cut out these people and put them into order of importance.
- Who was top Viking? Give reasons for your choices.

Male Slave

Lord

Lady

Farmer

Viking Time Line

- Match the pictures and labels correctly.
  Put them in time order.

THE Saxon King Alfred defeats Guthrum and his Viking army at Edington Wiltshire.

793 –

THE Normans, once Viking settlers in northern France, invade England.

866 –

A great Viking army invades. They settle in eastern England. Jorvik is their capital.

878 –

KING Ethelred pays the Vikings not to invade England.

1007 –

VIKING raiders attack and destroy the monastery on Lindisfarne.

1066 –

Using Living Things

- How did the Vikings use these creatures? Put them into the correct circle.

  Note that the circles overlap, so if a creature belongs to more than one circle, try to put them into the correct section of the circle.

- Explain how the creatures were used?

© 1995 Collins Educational

Viking Ships

We know from remains found buried that not all Viking ships were the same.

Here are some facts:

Warship: 18 metres long
2.6 metres wide

Trading vessel: 16.3 metres long
4.6 metres wide

Coastal ship: 23 metres long
5.5 metres wide

- Measure out the lengths of these ships on the playground.
- How did these ships move? How do we know?
- Try to build a model of a Viking ship.

Viking Warriors and Weapons

- Cut out these Viking warriors. Mount them in your book with the correct description of the weapon each is holding.

Clue: The Vikings usually gave their weapons and clothes names. Make up some names and descriptions of your own.

Battle Boar
does not speak in battle, but he makes a safe home for eyes to see.

Here am I,
Wolf of the Wound.
One blow is enough from my weighty iron tooth.

Sharp Heart Seeker
is my name. I may be small but my glittering bite is death.

My name is
Blade Eater.
Colourful wooden planks save the arm that holds me.

I am
Leg Biter.
I am long and iron strong. Magical patterns help me to deal death to my enemies.

Runes

Viking writing used straight lines so that it could easily be carved in wood or on stone.
The letters are called runes.
One alphabet had only 16 letters and it is called futhark.

- Can you see why?

F U TH A R K H N I A S T B M L R

The inscription on the stone says:

Harald the King set up this stone to his father, Gorm, and his mother Tyra. Harald won all Denmark and made the Danes Christian.

- Write a runic word of your own on the empty stone.

Children at Work and Play

- What are these Viking children doing?
- Which activity would children not do today?
- What might you do instead?

Viking Wallhanging: a Warrior

This tapestry hangs in a church in Norway. It shows one of the last Vikings wearing chain mail armour. He is like a warrior on another famous tapestry.

- Do you know which one?

- Colour this picture using only the original colours brown, mustard, grey, black, orange and white/cream.

Gods

Odin and Thor were the most important Viking gods.

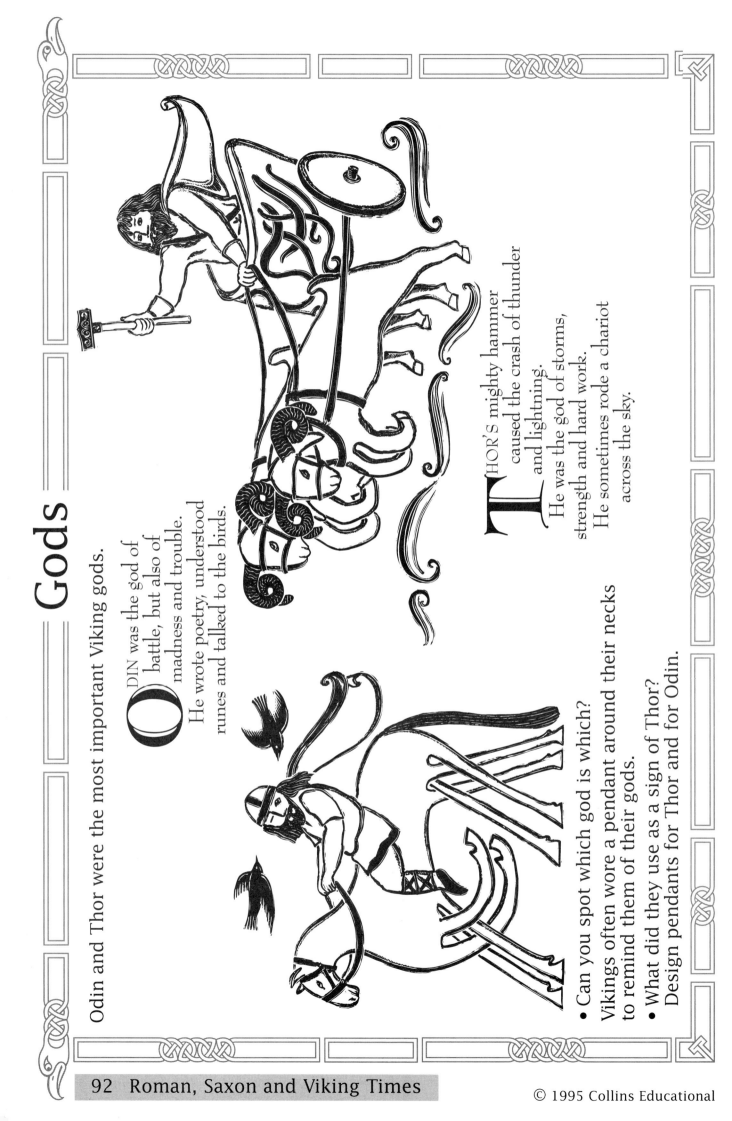

ODIN was the god of battle, but also of madness and trouble. He wrote poetry, understood runes and talked to the birds.

THOR'S mighty hammer caused the crash of thunder and lightning. He was the god of storms, strength and hard work. He sometimes rode a chariot across the sky.

- Can you spot which god is which?

Vikings often wore a pendant around their necks to remind them of their gods.

- What did they use as a sign of Thor? Design pendants for Thor and for Odin.

Viking Farm

This is a Viking farm that once existed in Yorkshire.

- Which is the main building?
- Which is the building used for cooking?
- Which is the workshop?

You can see inside one of the buildings.

- How did the Vikings make their houses warm and protect them from the weather?
- Make a list of instructions for building a Viking farmhouse.

Mystery Objects

- Be a detective.
  Match the labels and pictures.
  Explain what these mystery
  Viking objects might be.

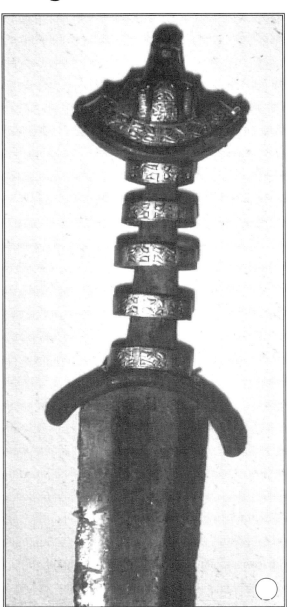

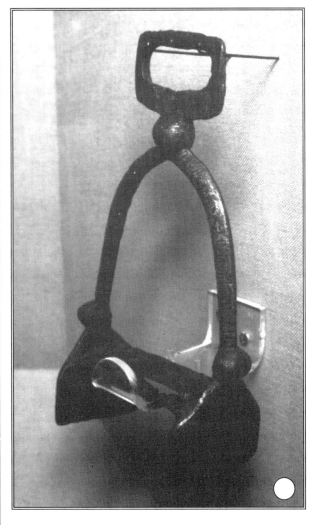

a iron with silver decoration
b iron with brass decoration
c iron
d silver

Bede's Book

Bede wrote a history of England.

• Can you tell from the picture what Bede was?

His writing may give you a clue:

THERE was a little boy in the monastery who had been seriously troubled by ague. He sat by St Oswald's tomb and the fever dared not touch him.

When St Oswald was killed his head was hacked off and placed on a stake. The following year Oswy came with his army and took the head to the church at Lindisfarne to be buried.

Two priests of the English race who had long lived in Ireland, went to the land of the Old Saxons to try to win them to Christ by their teaching. They had the same name but different coloured hair. One was known as Hewald the Black and the other Hewald the White.

You can buy a modern copy of Bede's History today.

• Design a suitable cover for his book.

Index